USDA

United States
Department of
Agriculture

Forest Service

Pacific Northwest
Research Station

General Technical
Report
PNW-GTR-823
November 2010

Evaluation of Native Plant Seeds and Seeding in the East-Side Central Cascades Ponderosa Pine Zone

Nan C. Vance

The **Forest Service** of the U.S. Department of Agriculture is dedicated to the principle of multiple use management of the Nation's forest resources for sustained yields of wood, water, forage, wildlife, and recreation. Through forestry research, cooperation with the States and private forest owners, and management of the National Forests and National Grasslands, it strives—as directed by Congress—to provide increasingly greater service to a growing Nation.

Author

Nan C. Vance is a research plant physiologist (emeritus), Forestry Sciences Laboratory, 3200 SW Jefferson Way, Corvallis, OR 97331.

All photographs by Nan Vance.

Abstract

Vance, Nan C. 2010. Evaluation of native plant seeds and seeding in the east-side central Cascades ponderosa pine zone. Gen. Tech. Rep. PNW-GTR-823. Portland, OR: U.S. Department of Agriculture, Forest Service, Pacific Northwest Research Station. 85 p.

In dry, open coniferous forests of the montane West, stand-replacing wildfires and land use activities alter the composition and abundance of native grasses and forbs by degrading the habitat and accelerating the invasion of exotic annuals. On these lands, native forbs and grasses delayed or prevented from recovery by natural processes may require intervention through supplementary seeding. However, effective seeding of native plants requires that their seed traits and the potential outcome of the seeding be better understood. This study evaluated seeds and seedlings of 13 native forbs and 5 grasses common in the dry *Pinus ponderosa/Purshia tridentata/ Festuca idahoensis* plant communities east of the Oregon Cascades crest and their potential for establishment in a landscape altered by past grazing and a recent, stand-replacing wildfire. Their potential for germination and establishment was examined in the laboratory and in 20 test plots located within the burned boundary of a 2002 wildfire. Seed collection, handling, testing, and sowing procedures are described. Data on seedling emergence, height, second-year survival and cover are presented in tables and figures. Onsite emergence and early growth data helped to reveal cause of early mortality related to biological and site conditions, including invasive competition, and differences in early growth and site occupancy. The study supports the efficacy of using multiple and functionally diverse species in a seeding program. Additional information on each of the 18 species is included in an appendix.

Keywords: Postfire rehabilitation, native forb, native grass, *Pinus ponderosa/ Purshia tridentata/Festuca idahoensis* plant association, seeds, seedlings, east-side central Oregon Cascades.

Preface

A series of executive orders and regulations by the USDA Forest Service recognize that sustainable ecosystems require the maintenance of native plant and animal diversity. The Forest Service Manual (FSM 2070) provides direction for the use, growth, development, and storage of native plant materials for revegetation, restoration, and rehabilitation of National Forest System lands to support its goal of protecting and conserving biological diversity. Inherent in this directive is the use of best available information for developing native plant materials most adapted to a site or situation; particularly in cases where natural regeneration sufficient to restore the native plant community is unlikely.

Contents

Introduction

Background

The dry montane forest zone where *Pinus ponderosa* is dominant or codominant is one of climatic extremes with shorter growing seasons and less annual precipitation than other forest zones (Franklin and Dyrness 1973, Simpson 2007). In Oregon, the *P. ponderosa* series forms a band along the east-side Oregon Cascade Range. In this band, even during the moist growing season from March through June, there are extreme fluctuations in temperature. Fire intervals in the *P. ponderosa* series were historically short and wildfires relatively light resulting in herbaceous vegetation dominating the understory. However, in recent years, wildfires occurring at longer intervals have tended to be larger and of higher severity (Agee 1994). In this semiarid ecosystem, recovery of the long-lived perennial grasses and forbs is slow even in plant communities highly adapted to periodic fire (Johnson 1998). However, sheep grazing, timber harvesting, and mechanized fire-control activities since the early 20th century (USDA FS 2004b), plus stand-replacing wildfires and spread of exotic annuals hinder the recovery or even irreversibly alter the native plant communities (Evans and Young 1978, Merriam et al. 2006, Monsen et al. 2004, Whisenant 1999).

Reduced grass cover and lack of shrub cover followed by severe wildfire removes almost any impediment to colonization by nonnative annual grasses, which, if they are present, will rapidly invade the postfire landscape (Arno 2000, Johnson 1998, Young and Evans 1978). In addition, seeding of annual and perennial nonnative grasses for postfire soil stabilization assumes that the germinated nonnative grasses would not persist after 2 years or be competitive with native species, and possibly, would function as a "nurse crop" for recolonizing native plants (USDA FS 2002). However, there is evidence to the contrary (Robichaud et al. 2000, Schoennagel and Waller 1999). Nonnative cereal grasses used in seeding for soil stabilization tend to persist, tend to interfere with the recovery of native plants, and do not prevent the almost inevitable expansion of exotic grasses and forbs if they are at all present in the area (Beyers 2004, Keeley 2004).

Wildland rehabilitation that is directed toward increasing the abundance of perennial native forbs and grasses should address the importance of diverse life forms and niche species. One goal of a rehabilitation plan might be to target keystone species and diverse functional groups. It should be emphasized, however, that sowing native forb and grass seeds on lands altered by severe wildfire will not re-create a prefire plant community. Fire and other disturbances owing to fire suppression activities may change soil, water, and light conditions irreversibly so that the trajectory of recovery goes in a different direction. In fact, successional changes that occur after a large fire often will include interim dominance of one or two species for years without the subsequent full recovery of native perennial plants (Johnson 1998).

Native forb and grass species appear to perform well in highly disturbed conditions where there is low nutrient availability, and thus could provide long-term resistance to annual bromes that tend to invade poorly occupied sites, especially following disturbance such as wildfire (Daehler 2003, Young and Evans 1978). Reintroducing a diverse mixture of native grasses and forbs may also help prevent or reduce the spread of noxious weeds along roads and in safety zones, dozer lines, and culvert replacement areas (Sheley and Half 2006, Tilman 1997). However, an impediment to restoring postfire plant communities or rehabilitating degraded landscapes is that the reproductive ecology, seed biology, and establishment requirements of many native flowering species and their symbionts are not well known, even those that are relatively common in fire-prone ecosystems of the Western United States. This lack of knowledge is one reason there is an increasing reliance on developing a small set of "performers" rather than striving for a diverse seed mix that would have greater potential to more fully occupy the landscape being rehabilitated. Unfortunately, the benefits of forb/grass mixes for seeding in dry forest types have not been proven, in part, because of the complexity introduced by differences among species in reproductive biology and site interactions that influence establishment rates (Jorgensen and Wilson 2004). Another approach thought to ensure enough established plants to inhibit invasive species establishment, is to sow at high density a seed mixture that includes aggressive, rapidly colonizing species (Sheley and Half 2006). A problem with that approach may be the potential for waste of costly seed and the suppression of desired perennials because of the colonizing success and later domination of one or a few aggressive, annual species (Brown and Amacher 1999, Brown and Rice 2000).

Study Objectives

This study sought to address the shortage of information on the differences in traits and characteristics among forb and grass species that might be used in developing a native plant seeding program. Specifically, this study sought to identify traits in 18 native perennial herbs and their associated environmental factors that affected germination success and early establishment in a postwildfire environment in the dry *Pinus ponderosa* plant association on the east-side central Oregon Cascade Range. Our approach was to study the seed biology and germination and early growth processes of selected species in a controlled seeding across a range of micro-conditions in spatially separated plots that would suggest whether they could be effectively used in rehabilitation programs. The approach involved first, collecting, cleaning, storing, and laboratory testing of seeds; second, evaluating germination in the field based on emergence; and third, measuring second-year survival and growth of seedlings. The outcome is detailed information on 18 species from seed through seedling. The data and discussions on performance in the field and laboratory may aid in developing rehabilitation strategies that use native plant seeds and help reduce costs by identifying important factors to consider in developing an appropriate mix of native forbs and grasses.

Species Assessment

The Site

Description—

The study site and seed collection area are located on 1300 ha (3,200 ac) of National Forest System land in Jefferson County, Oregon, under the management of the Deschutes National Forest, Sisters Ranger District. The site is on the easternmost flank of Green Ridge scarp in the Metolius River drainage and in a dry *Pinus ponderosa* series that extends along the eastern flank of the Cascade Range in a narrow band (fig. 1). The topography of the study area is primarily a gentle, east-facing slope (<15 percent) with an elevation gradient from 1000 m (3,200 ft) to 1100 m (3,600 ft) over 4.83 km (3 mi) in a southeast to northwest direction (fig. 2). The soils are characterized as moderate to shallow, sandy loam derived from ash-fall over basaltic colluvium and residuum of weathered tuff and andesite (USDA FS 2002). The forest type and plant association that best characterizes the study area is *Pinus ponderosa/Purshia tridentata/Festuca idahoensis* (PIPO/PUTR/FEID) in which *Pseudotsuga menziesii, Calocedrus decurrens*, and *Juniperus occidentalis* are occasional components of the understory (Franklin and Dyrness 1973). The most common members of the plant community based on our observations are listed in table 1.

Background conditions—

The Green Ridge study site is located within the perimeter of the July 2002 Eyerly wildfire, which burned about 9539 ha (23,573 ac) primarily on the Sisters Ranger District. The fire was of stand-replacement severity in 90 percent of the dry ponderosa pine plant association, which constituted 5188 ha (12,821 ac) (USDA FS 2004b). After the burn, a survey of about 44 km (27 mi) of dozer lines created during fire suppression indicated invasive exotics were present on about 70 percent of the surveyed lines (Suna and Van Campen 2003). Areas of high burn severity that lost root

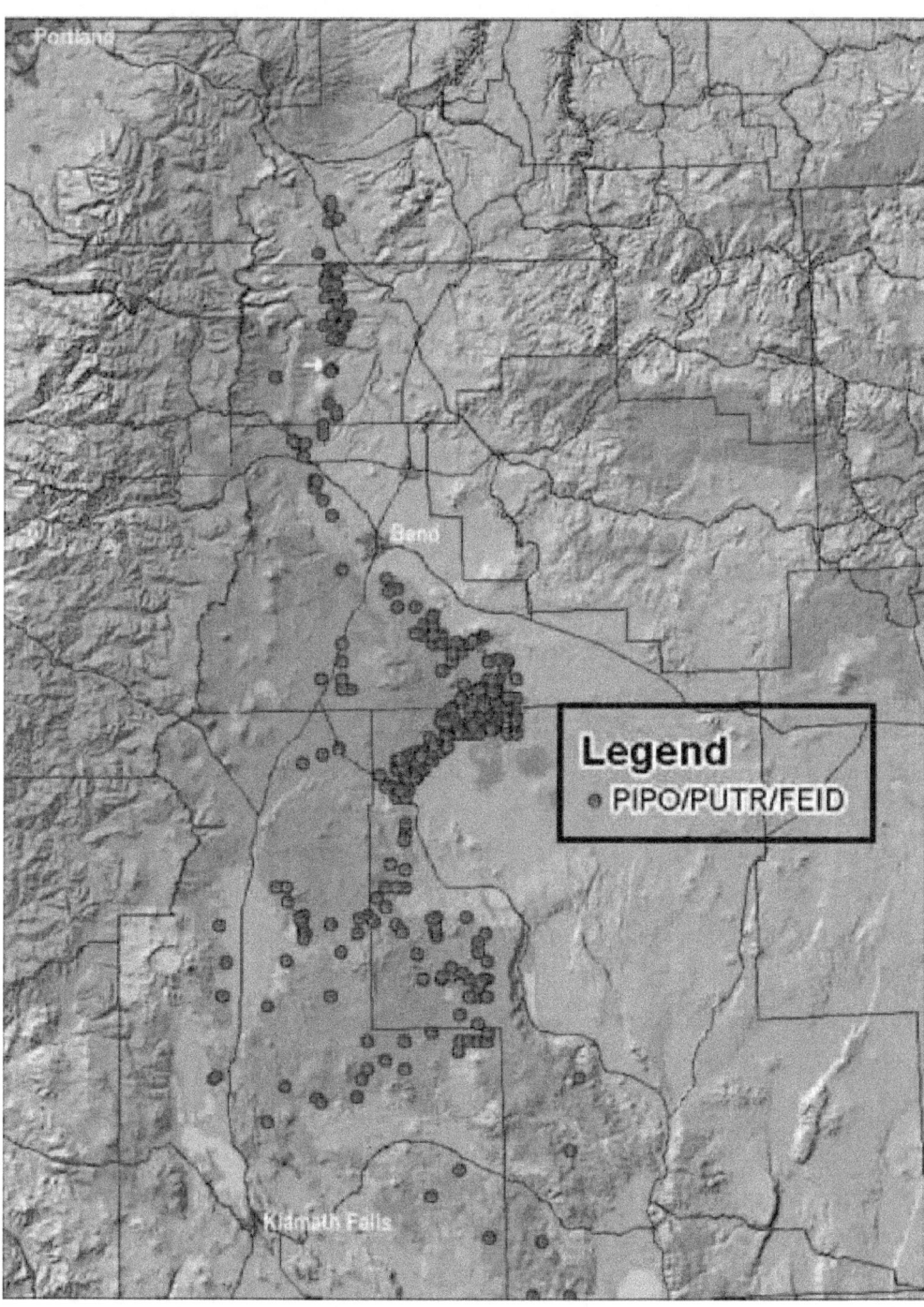

Figure 1—Locations of the *Pinus ponderosa/Purshia tridentata/Festuca idahoensis* (PIPO/PUTR/FEID) forest type in the central Oregon Cascade Range. Forest Service map with permission from Simpson (2007). White arrow shows study site.

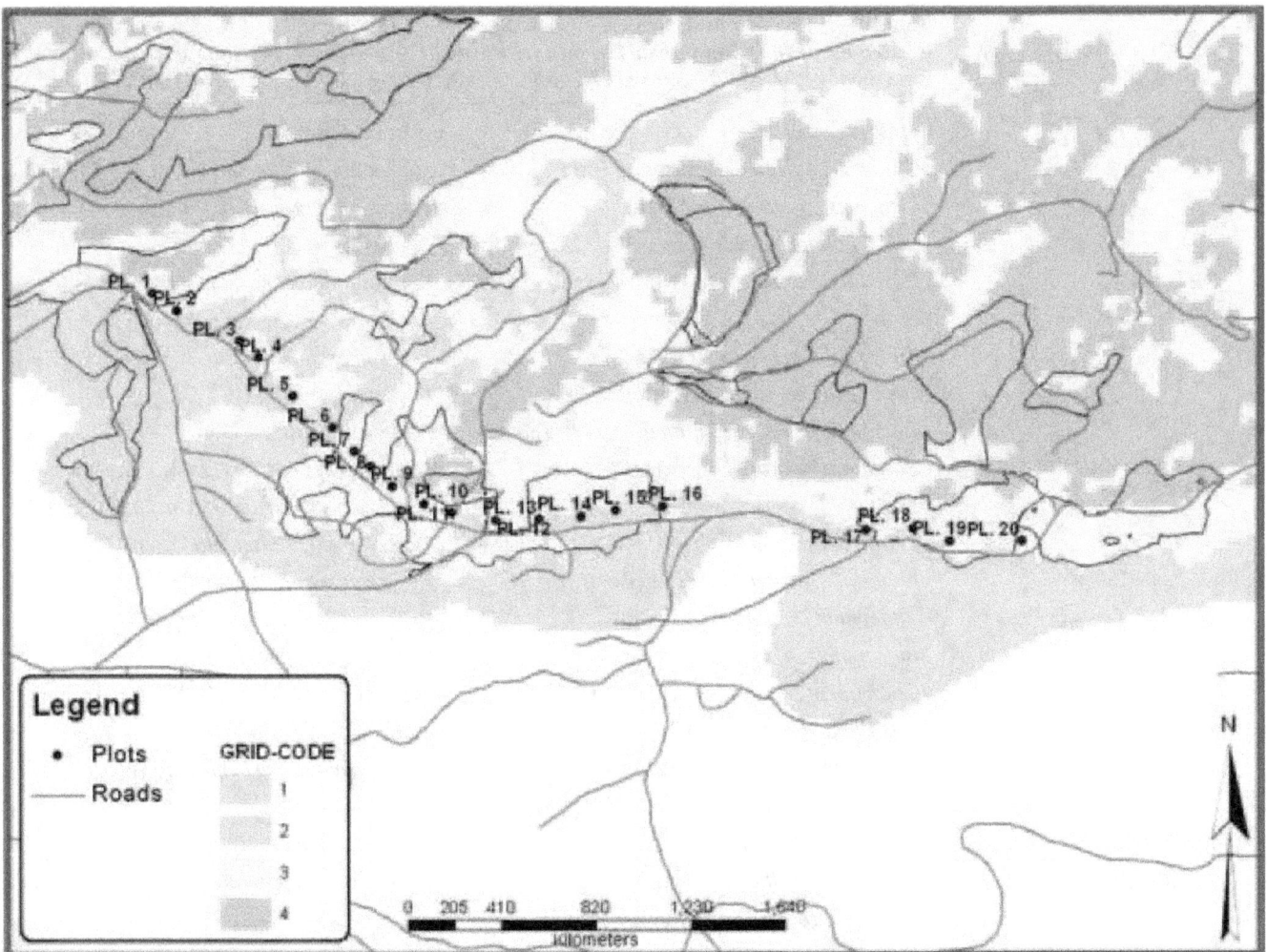

Figure 2—Positions of twenty 1-m^2 study plots for field seed germination/emergence tests on the Green Ridge site within the boundaries of the 2002 Eyerly wildfire. Map, courtesy of the Sisters Ranger District, Deschutes National Forest, includes roads and burn severity: 1, unburned; 2, low; 3, moderate; 4, high.

Table 1—Most common species observed growing in the vicinity of the 20 test plots located in a *Pinus ponderosa/Purshia tridentata/Festuca idahoensis* plant association at Green Ridge, east-side central Oregon Cascade Range

Trees:

   Calocedrus decurrens (Torr.) Florin

   Juniperus occidentalis Hook.

   Pinus ponderosa var. *ponderosa* C. Lawson

   Pseudotsuga menziesii (Mirb.) Franco

Shrubs:

   Arctostaphylos patula Greene

   Ceanothus prostratus Benth.

   Chrysothamnus viscidiflorus (Hook.) Nutt.

   Purshia tridentata (Pursh) DC.

Forbs:

   Achillea millefolium L.

   Anaphalis margaritacea L. (Benth.)

   Apocynum androsaemifolium L.

   Balsamorhiza careyana A. Gray

   Calochortus macrocarpus Dougl.

   Castilleja spp. Mutis ex L.

   Clarkia rhomboidea Dougl. ex Hook.

   Claytonia perfoliata Donn ex Willd.

   Claytonia sibirica L.

   Collinsia parviflora Dougl. ex Lindl.

   Collomia grandiflora Dougl. ex Lindl.

   Epilobium angustifolium L.

   Epilobium brachycarpum C. Presl.

   Epilobium minutum Lindl. ex Lehm.

   Eriogonum umbellatum Torr.

   Eriogonum spp. Michx.

   Eriophyllum lanatum (Pursh) Forbes

   Gayophytum diffusum Torr. & A. Gray

Forbs (continued)

   Hieracium albiflorum Hook.

   Lomatium nudicaule (Pursh.) Coult.
    & Rose

   Lomatium triternatum (Pursh.) Coult.
    & Rose

   Lotus crassifolius (Benth.) Greene

   Lupinus spp. L.

   Microseris spp. D. Don

   Microsteris gracilis (Hook.) Greene

   Navarretia divaricata (Torr. ex A. Gray)
    Greene ssp. *divaricata*

   Penstemon humilis Nutt. ex A. Gray

   Phacelia heterophylla Pursh

   Senecio triangularis Hook.

   Zigadenus venenosus S. Wats.

Graminoids:

   Achnatherum thurberianum (Piper)
    Barkworth

   Bromus tectorum L.

   Danthonia unispicata (Thurb.) Munro
    ex Macoun

   Elymus elymoides (Raf.) Swezey

   Festuca idahoensis Elmer

   Koeleria macrantha (Ledeb.) J.A.
    Schultes

   Poa bulbosa L.

   Poa secunda J. Presl.

   Pseudoroegneria spicata (Pursh.) A. Love

stock and seed sources were described as "highly susceptible to invasion by noxious weeds and other nonnative invasives." Populations of noxious weeds in areas disturbed in the fire suppression activities were found to have spread into areas previously not infested (USDA FS 2002). The most prevalent of the species were the opportunistic, nonnative annual grasses medusahead (*Taeniatherum caput-medusae* [L.] Nevski) and cheatgrass (*Bromus tectorum*), and the forb, spotted knapweed (*Centaurea maculosa* Lam.). Almost all sites were identified as high risk for spread by these species (USDA FS 2002). Since then, the spread boundary and density of weeds have increased (Suna and Van Campen 2003).

During the fall of 2002, in accordance with Forest Service guidelines for Burned Area Emergency Response (BAER) (FSH 2509-13), the steep, north-facing slope north of the study area on Green Ridge was aerially seeded with "sterile" winter wheat (*Triticum aestivum* L. [Madsen]) and annual ryegrass (*Lolium perenne* L. ssp. *multiflorum* (Lam.) Husnot [Gulf]) at a rate of 215 pure live seeds (pls)/m^2 (20 pls/ft^2). The seeding extended beyond the slope about 50 m onto the ridgetop. Factors in the decision to seed with nonnative grasses were low cost and "lack of availability of suitable native species." The sterile winter wheat and rye formed dense patches in 2004–2005 and began encroaching into the study area. Four years after the burn in May and June, part of the study area was salvage logged to remove dead and severely damaged trees using skyline and helicopter yarding (USDA FS 2002).

Throughout most of the burn zone on the top of Green Ridge, *Bromus tectorum* and other nonnative grass species were visible as scattered individuals and small patches having migrated upslope from adjacent sagebrush steppe lands. Where heavy equipment was used to make fire lanes or for tree removal, the ground was scarified to bare mineral soil. Appearing for the first time in these disturbed soils were exotic, annual forbs possibly introduced in the commercial grass-seed mix (Forcella and Harvey 1983, Miller et al. 1999). However, the fire-opened stands of pine also increased soil exposure with loss of ground vegetation, which may have favored the spread of annual grasses such as *T. caput-medusa, B. tectorum,* and *Vulpia* spp. (Merriam et al. 2006, Miller et al. 1999, Mosely et al. 1999, Wilderman 2003).

Seed Evaluations

Field survey and collection—

Before collecting seeds in 2004, we made a preliminary list of forb and grass species considered appropriate for reintroduction aided by the Deschutes National Forest's species list, a review of published literature, and a preliminary field survey of the most common species growing in the PIPO/PUTR/FEID plant association at or near the site. We surveyed for potential seed collection areas and identified species that were sufficiently abundant in neighboring unburned areas to furnish an adequate amount of seed for the study, then mapped them. The potential seed-collection area comprised about 5180 ha (12,800 ac) on Green Ridge adjacent to and including forested lands burned in the Eyerly Fire. To observe species in flower, we made several visits to the area in spring and early summer. We confined our seed collection areas to the PIPO/PUTR/FEID plant association so that we would not include offsite species. We selected species for collection based on their potential seed availability, early establishment and growth, site occupancy, and representation of forest type. We chose not to collect species, such as *Achillea millefolium*, that are cosmopolitan and putative increasers after fire and for which there appeared to be an adequate seed source (Johnson 1998). These 5 grass and 13 forb species met our criteria: *Elymus elymoides, Festuca idahoensis, Achnatherum thurberianum, Poa secunda, Pseudoroegnaria spicata, Apocynum androsaemifolium, Balsamorhiza careyana, Calochortus macrocarpus, Erigeron filifolius* (Hook.) Nutt. var. *filifolius, Eriogonum umbellatum, Eriophyllum lanatum, Linum lewisii, Lomatium triternatum, Lotus crassifolius, Olsynium douglasii* (A. Dietr.) E.P. Bicknell, *Penstemon humilus, Silene douglasii* Hook., and *Zigadenus venenosus*.

The seeds from plants of locally identified species were hand collected on different dates depending on their phenology of flowering, fruiting, and seed maturation. From July through September 2004, while we collected seeds for field testing, we noted condition of fruits or seeds including fullness, maturity, and insect or other predation, as well as dates and appearance of fruit or seed maturity. All collected seeds and fruits were placed in labeled paper bags and stored in the shade in dry conditions until they were cleaned. Collection procedures for each species can be found in the appendix. We also collected individual plants for pressing and taxonomic identification at the Oregon State University herbarium. Identification of grass species was aided by Dr. Paul Doescher, Department of Rangeland Resources, Oregon State University.

Seeds were not co-mingled with seeds in other collection bags until each was carefully examined for insect-infested seeds to avoid cross contamination. For each species, we kept collections separate as numbered seed lots if the interval between collections was greater than 1 week or if the collection location was separated by more than 2.0 km (1.3 mi) until we determined if differences in collection date or location affected viability.

Seed cleaning—
Seeds were collected and cleaned in 2004 and 2005. The seeds were cleaned by hand mechanically using screens and air separators tailored to most efficiently clean

seeds of each species (Douglas et al. 1997). Slightly different processing equipment was used in each year although the overall approach for each species was the same (Harmond et al. 1968). In 2004, we used the seed cleaning facility of the USDA Agricultural Research Service laboratory on the Oregon State University campus, Corvallis, Oregon. The first stage of the process was to remove awns from grass seed and extraneous material from the forb seeds. In 2004, we used a Westrup[1] brush machine consisting of a mesh wire cylinder and two rotating brushes (Barbour 2002). In 2005, at the USDA Forest Service Bend Seed Extractory in Bend, Oregon, we used a Clipper air screen separator (USDA FS 2006b). The Westrup brush machine or Clipper air screen separator was used in the initial cleaning stages on all five grass species and for seeds of *Eriophylum lanatum* and *Lomatium triternatum*. For seeds of other forbs such as *Balsamorhiza careyana*, fruit or seed heads were crushed by hand or with a crushing boat, and screened. The fine chaff and empty seeds were removed by carefully blowing with controlled, forced air. Through mechanical cleaning and blowing, we removed almost all of the inert matter including broken and empty seeds. The cleaned seeds were placed in paper envelopes identified and labeled according to species and source, which were then held in cold/dry storage. The specific methods that were applied to seeds of each species are reported in the appendix.

Filled seed—

In 2004, we estimated the amount of filled seed in our collections by sampling seeds from our collection bags before samples were mechanically cleaned. For grass species, we used back-lighted trays to help determine empty or damaged caryopses. We also inspected cut seed using a dissecting microscope to examine the embryo and endosperm using the *Handbook on Seeds of Browse-Shrubs and Forbs* as a guide (AOSA 2003a). The percentage of filled seeds differed among lots of the same species. Some seed lots appeared affected by predators as they had more visibly insect-damaged seeds than others. Herbaceous plants are known to vary spatially and temporally in seed production and abundance (Apfelbaum et al. 1997). Estimating this variability would be useful for calculating how much collecting effort is needed to acquire a given amount of good seed.

Because fecundity of a plant species greatly influences the availability of seeds, determining intra-specific variation in filled seed would aid in developing a seed collection strategy. The percentage of filled seed is also a measure of a species' reproductive fitness. In 2005, we introduced a sampling scheme so that we

---

[1] The use of trade or firm names in this publication is for reader information and does not imply endorsement by the U.S. Department of Agriculture of any product or service.

could calculate percentage of filled seed from a known number of fruiting units. To ensure that the range of environmental adaptation to the site was genetically represented, we stratified the collection area into five subareas for collecting fruits of 14 species in a stratified random design. We gathered fruits of each of 14 species from four randomly selected plants in each of the subareas. All seeds were carefully removed from the seed head or fruit and counted. We recorded filled, empty, and damaged seed from individual or multiple fruits, depending on the species, using the method previously described. All caryopses of the grasses in the panicle or spike of a single stem were counted. Seed heads were the fruit unit for species of the Asteraceae family, and the umbel for *Eriogonum umbellatum* (3 to 8 seed heads/umbel) and *Lomatium triternatum* (9 to 16 umbellate seed "heads" of a compound umbel). For *Linum lewisii*, *Silene douglasii*, and *Penstemon humilis*, as well as the liliaceous monocots, a capsule was the fruiting unit.

The filled-seed data were analyzed by analysis of variance (ANOVA). Each species was analyzed independently. For five of the species, filled-seed data that did not meet the assumptions for ANOVA were analyzed by the nonparametric Kruskal-Wallis (1952) one-way analysis of variance, (the Kruskal-Wallis statistic H and the ANOVA statistic F agreed at $P \leq 0.05$ level of confidence). Because the medians of the species nonparametrically tested for variance were close in value to the means, means are shown for all species in table 2.

Variability in filled seed was high among the fruits within each species in 2005 and greater among sampled individuals of a species within each subarea than among subareas for most species. Despite the high variability among individuals, a significant difference in average filled seeds ($P < 0.05$) among subareas was detected in *L. triternatum*, *S. douglasii*, *Poa secunda,* and *Pseudoroegnaria spicata*. The causes of the differences were not identified, but spatial variation in fecundity within a large population or seed collection area has implications for developing a seed collection strategy that seeks to gather not only quantity but as much quality seed as possible.

Although the mean filled-seed rate of many species differed between years (table 2), data were not compared statistically, because in 2004 the percentage of filled seed was calculated on seeds drawn from seed lots representing a variable number of plants. In 2005, seeds were collected from fruiting units on only four randomly selected plants per subarea. However, the seeds both years came from the same seed collecting area. In 2004, chaff had been removed from the seeds of *Balsamorhiza careyana*, *L. lewisii* and *S. douglasii* by hand screening before a sample was drawn from the bags; nevertheless, the filled-seed rate of *L. lewisii* both years was 100 percent, consistent with high percentages of germination reported by

Table 2—Filled-seed percentage of seeds collected in 2004 (pooled seed) and 2005 (directly from plants) of 5 grasses and 13 forbs growing in an approximately 26-km^2 (10-mi^2) area at the Green Ridge study site in the east-side central Oregon Cascade Range

Species	2004	2005
	Percent	
Grasses:		
Achnatherum thurberianum	60.0	61.6
Elymus elymoides	75.0	81.8
Festuca idahoensis	47.0	40.5
Poa secunda	35.0	33.2
Pseudoroegnaria spicata	33.3	22.6
Forbs:		
Apocynum androsaemifolium	54.0	N.d.
Balsamorhiza careyana[a]	48.9	8.7
Calohortus macrocarpus	90.0	47.0
Erigeron filifolius	45.0	11.6
Eriogonum umbellatum	71.7	17.3
Eriophyllum lanatum	71.0	57.8
Linum lewisii[a]	100.0	100.0
Lomatium triternatum	73.3	86.5
Lotus crassifolius	73.3	60.3
Olsynium douglasii	88.9	N.d.
Penstemon humilis	83.3	N.d.
Silene douglasii[a]	100.0	78.0
Zigadenus venenosus	82.2	N.d.

Note: For 2004 seeds, Number of lots tested ranged from 1 to 6; for 2005, N = 5; N.d. = no data.
[a] Seeds in 2004 were previously hand cleaned.

Meyer and Kitchen (1994). The filled-seed rate of *B. careyana* was low in 2004 and was much lower in 2005 (table 2). The seed heads of *B. careyana* plants collected in 2005 were fewer in number, frequently appeared damaged, and were smaller than those collected in 2004 indicating that the reduction in filled seed probably was not due to hand cleaning the seeds. In 2005, ungulates browsed the fruiting stalks of *Calochortus macrocarpus*; from the appearance of the browsed plants, the browsers selected taller stems bearing larger capsules. We noticed smaller plants remained with smaller fruit having fewer filled seeds than fruit in 2004. Other forb species also appeared to have lower filled-seed rates in 2005 for which we have no explanation. However, reported differences in rate of filled seed between years have been related to corresponding differences between years in temperature and precipitation during seed development (Valencia-Diaz and Montaña 2005).

Seed collecting in the wild would be more effective if estimation of seed collection time and effort included not only spatial distribution and density of flowering plants, but also the plant's fecundity or rate of seed production. Being able to estimate seed productivity would increase efficiency by providing a better estimate of how many flowering plants are needed for seed. Parameters that may help in estimating seed productivity are ratio of fruit-to-flower, total number of seeds, and percentage of filled seeds per individual. If plants in a collection area have a high yield of seed, then collection intensity might be reduced. In addition, if plant fecundity is found to differ within a large collection area, it is important that the collection area be appropriately represented. It is safe to suggest that the inter-play of biological, genetic, and environmental factors that influence seed production may also produce ecotypic variation that is spatially distributed in seed traits among populations or colonies (Erickson et al. 2004, Linhart 1995).

Seed weight—

As the number of seeds per unit weight is influenced by a seed's moisture content, we calculated the moisture content of seeds at time of weighing. Collected seeds were left in open paper bags in the laboratory for 1 week before they were weighed to ensure that seeds were sufficiently dry and their weight was stable. To determine moisture content, a representative sample of seeds was weighed, dried in a labora-tory oven at 65 °C (149 °F) for 24 h, equilibrated with room temperature in a desic-cator, then reweighed. This procedure was repeated for another 24 h at a drying temperature of 105 °C (221 °F). After the second drying, relative moisture content was calculated on a wet-weight basis. Seed number per unit weight was calculated for each species using cleaned seeds having moisture content ranging from 5.8 to 9.9 percent (table 3).

We determined number of seeds per kilogram (pound) for each species by calculating the mean weight in grams of three replicates of 50, 100, and 200 ran-domly sampled seeds with weight recorded to 0.0001 g. Mean weight was linearly regressed against the counted seeds to generate the number of seeds per unit weight (grams). The coefficient of variation (r^2) of each regression was > 0.99 for seeds of every species. The number of seeds per kilogram and per pound is shown in table 3. For some species, the rate deviated from published data (Hassell et al. 1996, Lam-bert 2005, Monsen and Stevens 2004). For example, the mean number of seeds per pound of *L. lewisii* seeds that were collected at Green Ridge was 152,095, but as many as 278,000 to 420,000 seeds per pound were reported in *Seeding Rate Statistics for Native and Introduced Species* by Hassell et al. (1996). Such discrep-ancies may be due to differences in purity of the seed lot and moisture content of the seeds, resources for seed development, seed predation, or genetic-based differ-ences among varieties in seed size or mass (Cavers and Steel 1984, Thompson and

Table 3—Number per unit weight of cleaned, filled seeds of 18 native plant species at the relative moisture content indicated (ambient temperature 22 to 25 °C)

Species	Seeds/kg	Seeds/lb	Seed moisture	TZ	Seed lots
	No.	*No.*	*%*	*%*	*No.*
Grasses:					
Achnatherum thurberianum	485,950	220,886	9.9	92	3
Elymus elymoides	190,440	86,564	9.7	92	2
Festuca idahoensis	676,050	307,295	9.2	83	3
Poa secunda	1,655,800	752,182	8.8	69	2
Pseudoroegneria spicata	267,790	121,723	9.3	87	2
Forbs:					
Apocynum androsaemifolium	2,684,700	1,220,318	—	55	1
Balsamorhiza careyana	93,130	42,332	7.8	79	2
Calochortus macrocarpus	377,010	171,368	–	86	1
Erigeron filifolius	5,301,900	2,409,955	7.2	85	2
Eriogonum umbellatum	291,000	132,245	8.8	73	2
Eriophyllum lanatum	1,387,900	630,864	5.6	59	2
Linum lewisii	334,610	152,095	5.9	97	1
Lomatium triternatum	145,160	65,982	7.9	77	1
Lotus crassifolius	88,230	40,105	7.9	95	2
Olsynium douglasii	293,460	133,391	—	79	1
Penstemon humilis	4,822,100	2,191,864	—	88	1
Silene douglasii	1,523, 700	692,591	9.3	90	2
Zigadenus venenosus	285,770	129,895	—	86	2

Note: Seeds were tested for viability using tetrazolium (TZ) at Oregon State University Seed Laboratory. Percentage of viability shown is the mean of the lots unless a single lot was used.

Pellmyr 1989, Tyson 1989). For example, the *Linum* cultivar "Appar" has significantly lighter seeds than interior northwestern ecotypes of the native *L. lewisii* (Pendleton et al. 2008).

Physiological tests—

Approximately 200 cleaned seeds from collections of each species were tested for viability at the Oregon State University Seed Testing Laboratory, Corvallis, Oregon, using Association of Official Seed Analysts (AOSA) protocols (AOSA 2003b, Peters 2000). The test included quantification of filled or abnormal seed, and a chemical test for metabolic activity by means of tetrazolium (TZ) salts color analysis (Peters 2000). A viability test was run on each lot and is presented as the mean percentage of the lots that were pooled for use in the in vitro germination tests as well as in the field evaluation (table 3).

Seeds in long-term storage should be stored at low temperatures and at a sufficiently low moisture content to maintain dormancy, hold respiration to a minimum, and inhibit microbial activity (Iriondo and Perez 1999, Jorgensen and

Wilson 2004, Young and Young 1986). For approximately 6 months, seeds stored dry in paper bags were kept in a walk-in cooler. Seeds of grasses were not stratified. In mid January, seeds of forbs receiving 10-week stratification were placed in cheesecloth, soaked 24 h under running water in mesh bags, and stored in filter paper in a walk-in cooler for 10 weeks. Although the thermostat in the cooler was set for temperatures that ranged from 2 to 4 °C (36 to 39 °F), the temperatures after the first week were found to be ranging from approximately 4 to 6 °C (39 to 43 °F). The seeds of *Eriophylum lanatum, Eriogonum umbellatum, Silene douglasii,* and *Zigadenus venenosus* germinated in the cooler with some appearing moldy. Many of the ungerminated seeds of *Apocynum androsaemifolium* were also moldy (74 percent). The seeds were moved to a different cooler in which the temperature was 3.9 °C ± 1° (38.0 °F ± 1°); but the germination test was compromised for these species. Five replicates of 50 seeds each for each species that could be tested, including the unstratified grass seeds, were rinsed, placed on moistened filter paper in a labeled petri dish, and placed in a growth chamber set to a 12-h, day/night thermoperiod of 18/10 °C (64/50 °F). Seeds were counted every day or every 2 days for up to 10 weeks. Seeds that germinated and acquired mold were recorded and removed. Because *Lotus crassifolius* is a leguminous species with a putative impermeable seed coat, different treatments were applied including stratification with a 48- or 24-h pre-soak, and with light scarification (using sandpaper) or no scarification. The no-stratification treatment had a 48-h pre-soak and scarification only. Each treatment replicated five times was applied to seeds of *L. crassifolius* that were germinated as described above. The treatments were statistically tested for treatment differences by ANOVA.

The mean germination percentage of unstratified seeds of *L. crassifolius* with 48-h soak and scarification was significantly lower ($P < 0.05$) than the germination of stratified seeds with additional soak and scarification treatments. Among the stratified seeds, the longer (48-h) soak and scarification significantly improved germination (table 4). Our results agreed with those reported by the USDA Natural Resources Conservation Service, Corvallis Plant Materials Center (Flessner and Darris 2001). The mean germination percentage of all grass species was 75.9 percent (*Poa secunda* was not included in the test). However, seed germination rates of stratified seeds of the forbs were lower than their potential to germinate as indicated by the viability tests (table 3, table 4).

Some species' germination requirements apparently were not met by the procedures we used. For example, none of the *Linum lewisii* seeds germinated even though filled-seed and viability percentages were high. Seed germination might have improved under lower temperatures and an 8-h day/16-h night,

Table 4—Germination of grass and forb seeds collected from Green Ridge, Deschutes National Forest, with or without 10-week stratification

Species	Stratification	Germination	Mold
		– – – Percent – – –	
Grasses:			
Achnatherum thurberianum	+	64.8	8.0
Elymus elymoides	–	82.8	7.2
Festuca idahoensis	–	80.8	9.2
Pseudoroegneria spicata	–	75.2	9.6
Forbs:			
Apocynum androsaemifolium	+	28.0	74.7
Balsamorhiza careyana	+	9.6	8.8
Erigeron filifolius	+	35.3	16.0
Eriogonum umbellatum	–	37.2	42.4
Linum lewisii	+	0.0	1.8
Lomatium triternatum	+	16.0	1.5
Lotus crassifolius			
Scarification, 48 h soak	–	0.4a	2.0
No scarification, 48 h soak	+	29.6b	1.2
Scarification, 48 h soak	+	43.2c	0.8
No scarification, 24 h soak	+	29.6b	0.4
Scarification, 24 h soak	+	32.8bc	0.4

Note: Seeds were germinated in the laboratory under standard light and temperature. Additional treatments were applied to seeds of *Lotus crassifolius* only. Letters indicate significant differences among treatments at $P \leq 0.05$, N = 5.

which mimics the short day length of spring/fall when most seeds of these species naturally germinate (Beckstead et al. 1995, Goodwin et al. 1996, Young and Evans 1979). Drake et al. (1998) reported that outdoor germination under natural conditions appeared to improve germination, which suggests that test conditions more closely approximating those of the seeds' native conditions may improve test results.

For optimal results, in vitro seed germination test conditions at a minimum should be species specific and ideally based on the physiological seed and dormancy requirements that may occur among different ecotypes. Seed dormancy and germination requirements have been found to differ not only among species but among ecotypes and populations within a species (Doescher et al. 1985, Erickson et al. 2004, Goodwin et al. 1996, Meyer and Kitchen 1994). The germination of *L. lewisii* seeds from the intermountain West ranged from 0 to 100 percent depending on their origins, dormancy requirements, ability to after-ripen, and genotype (Jorgensen and Wilson 2004, Meyer and Kitchen 1994). Dormancy and initiation of seed germination also may be influenced by elevation, latitude, and climatic patterns of the population's origins (Beckstead et al. 1995, Cavieres and Arroyo 2000). Seeds of perennial, vernal herbs and grasses able to germinate in cold soil at elevations of about 1000 m (3,280 ft) or lower may require shorter periods of stratification than species adapted to higher elevations (Cavieres and Arroyo 2000). The native grasses *Elymus elymoides, Festuca idahoensis, Poa secunda, and Pseudoroegnaria spicata* adapted to the elevation and climate of Green Ridge or other similar environments in the ponderosa pine zone east of the Cascades summit may not require stratification; their germination phenology at midelevations or lower may be dictated more by precipitation patterns (Beckstead et al. 1995, Goodwin et al. 1995).

Species' Performance on Site

Site preparation and sowing—

In September 2004, the study plots were located on the easternmost extension of Green Ridge within the southeastern edge of the Eyerly Fire boundary. Twenty plots were installed transecting the southern burn boundary and spanning about 5 km or 3 mi (fig. 2). Each 1-m^2 plot was located 50 m from the road and a minimum distance of 150 m from each other. Part of the 5-km transect intercepted an unburned area from which plots were excluded.

In each 1-m^2 plot, sixteen 15- by 15-cm (6- by 6-in) and two 4- by 60-cm (2- by 24-in) subplots were prepared for seeding by clearing off thatch and debris, and lightly raking the surface. Four furrows about 15 cm long and 4 cm apart were prepared for each of the 16 subplots, and a single furrow about 60 cm long was prepared for the two additional species. Each long subplot had a minimum of 5 cm (2 in) between its furrow and that of any other subplot so that no seeded furrow was closer than 5 cm from another, within or between species. The species were randomly assigned a subplot in each of the 20 plots with the exception of *Calochortus macrocarpus* and *Penstemon humilis,* which were randomly assigned to one of the 4- by 60-cm plots.

Where there was more than one seed lot available, two or more lots of each species were combined equally by weight based on lot size, percentage purity, and TZ test results. Fifty seeds of each species having relatively large seeds and 100 seeds of each grass species and forb species having smaller seeds were counted and replicated 20 times. The seeds were sown individually by hand in late September at a depth of 1.0 to 1.5 cm (0.4 to 0.6 in) depending on seed size of the species. Soil was smoothed over the seeds and gently tamped down. We used no mulch for cover; however, chicken wire was firmly secured over the plots to protect the seeds from large animal disturbance (fig. 3A). The plots were marked at each corner and oriented toward the north for consistent reference and relocation.

Figure 3—(A) One of twenty study plots installed at Green Ridge, Deschutes National Forest to evaluate native plant seed germination, seedling emergence, and survival. (B) *Eriogonum umbellatum* germinant emerging in early March with anthocyanin pigment visible on hypocotyl and cotyledon. (C) Frost heaving caused grass seeds sown 1.0 to 1.5 cm below ground to germinate on the surface of the soil. (D) Soil surface of plot 2 that reached temperatures > 50 °C; the herb *Navarretia divaricata* ssp. *divaricata* adapted to survive those conditions. (E) A *Lotus crassifolius* seedling that has been predated by insect larvae. (F) A study plot with vegetative cover consisting primarily of the invasive annual grass *Bromus tectorum*.

We measured relative light over the plot using a LI-COR LAI-2000 Plant Canopy Analyzer (LI-COR Inc. Lincoln, NE). The plant canopy analyzer estimates exposure of plot relative to full irradiance by calculating a ratio of nonintercepted diffused light (DIFN) measured on plot points to a fixed point receiving full light. Five calculations of DIFN were averaged from filtered solar irradiance readings 1.0 m (3.3 ft) above ground at plot center and at each plot corner. We installed sensors for collecting microclimate data (models GPSE 301 203, A.R. Harris Ltd.

Christchurch, New Zealand) near plots that would best represent the range of moisture and temperatures in the transect. The sensors were positioned to measure air temperature and relative humidity 50 cm above the ground and soil temperature at rooting level 3.0 to 4.0 cm (1.2 to 1.6 in) below ground. Before the plots were prepared for sowing, we recorded moss, forb, and grass cover and soil exposure. We also recorded the most commonly occurring plants that were present in the plot and up to 3 m outside the plot perimeter, and recorded the presence of *Bromus tectorum* outside and within the plot.

Emergence of shoots or cotyledons was used as a measure of successful seed germination. Because vernal herbs only grow and reproduce in the spring, we recorded emergence beginning in February 2005. Cumulative emergence was tallied for each species in each of the 18 subplots 20 times at intervals of 3 to 4 weeks through May 2005 when there was no visible new emergence. We calculated mean germination of each species as the mean of the highest number of emergent seedlings recorded in each of the 20 plots from February through April 2005 (N = 20). Mean percentage of survival was calculated from the recorded number of living seedlings in May and June 2005, and May 2006. When seedlings were of sufficient height ($\geq$ 1 cm), we also measured the length of the five longest leaves or shoots of selected individuals in each subplot; otherwise we noted if they were < 1 cm. In addition, we recorded the percentage of exposed soil, moss, and vegetative cover, and separately, cover of the 18 study species in the plots. We also recorded presence of invasive species, and noted visible predation, disease, or injury. Data in May 2006 were taken under drier conditions than May 2005 (Oregon Climate Service 2009). Leaves, especially of the monocots, had begun senescing in May 2006, so percentage of their cover may have been underestimated.

Statistical analysis to compare differences between years for each species was by paired t-test on repeated measures for survival and cover. Where assumptions of equal variance were not met, the nonparametric Mann-Whitney-Wilcoxon test of differences between medians was used (α = 0.05). Regression analysis was used to examine relations between variables.

Field environment—

Diurnal soil temperatures in February and March fluctuated above and below freezing. Soil temperature at night near the surface and within the rooting zone was lower than if there had been an insulating snow layer. However, the anthocyanic pigments visible in the cotyledons and hypocotyls (fig. 3B) suggest they are cold tolerant if not freezing tolerant (Close et al. 2004, McKown et al. 1996). Lack of snow cover also promoted cycles of freeze and thaw in the soil that cause "frost heaving," a dynamic microtopography that, depending upon root length and seed size or position, either buries, shelters, or exposes germinating seeds to temperature extremes. This phenomenon was particularly evident in plots with little canopy or vegetative cover (fig. 3C). Frost heaving contributed to reducing the rate of emergence and survival of some of the small-seeded and grass species, as dead germinants were observed on the soil surface. However, their mortality in relation to frost-heaving could not be quantified.

The DIFN on the 20 plots ranged from 0.52 to 0.96 on plots with moderate shade to near total exposure. The monthly mean soil temperatures of plots highly exposed to solar irradiance were higher in spring and summer than those of the more shaded plots. For example, the fully exposed plot 2 (figs. 4C, 3D) had greater fluctuations in soil temperature than the partially shaded plot 18 (fig. 4B). By July, the mean maximum soil temperature in exposed plot 2 exceeded 50 °C and was almost 10 degrees higher than the shaded plot 18 (fig. 4 C, D). Soil surface temperatures > 50 °C can be lethal to newly emergent seedlings and may have contributed to high mortality in those plots (Wickens 1998). Note that the dominant species on

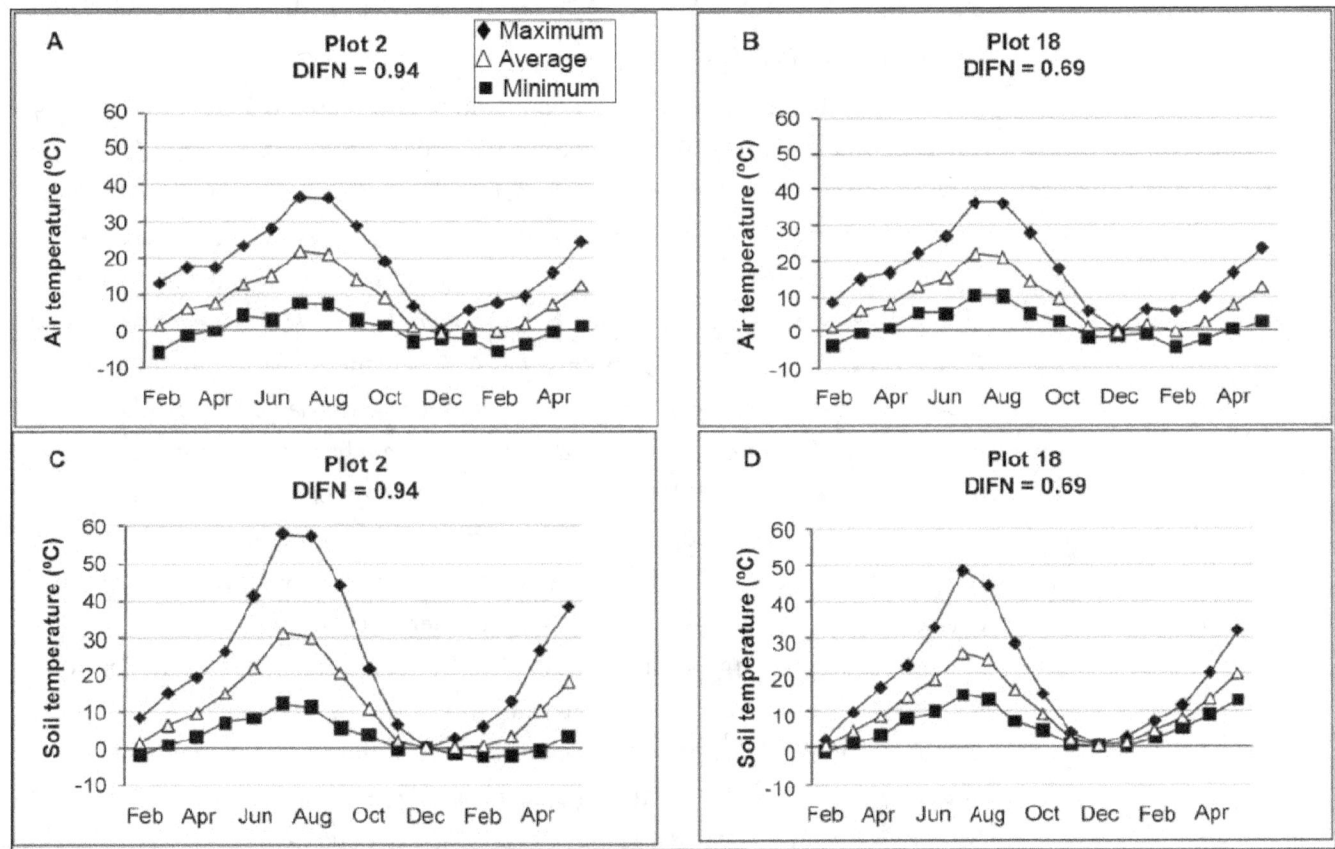

Figure 4—Mean monthly air and soil temperatures from the high, low, and average diurnal temperatures taken by data loggers from February 2005 through May 2006 installed adjacent to plot 2 (A,C) and plot 18 (B,D), which had different levels of direct sunlight, (nonintercepted diffuse light [DIFN] = 0.94 and 0.69, respectively).

the otherwise depauperate plot 2 was *Navarretia divaricata* ssp. *divaricata,* an herb of the dry West structurally adapted to avoid tissue damage from lethal soil surface temperatures in semiarid climate (fig. 3D).

The mean percentage of exposed soil and cover of moss and herbaceous vegetation on the 20 plots differed temporally as well as spatially. Nonvegetated soil declined from 78 percent in 2004 to 65 percent in 2006 as moss and herbaceous cover correspondingly increased. Moss cover increased from 3 percent in 2004, (range, 0 to 15 percent) to 23 percent in 2006 (range, 0 to 80 percent). There was no linear relation between percentage of seedling emergence on plots and moss cover, and no direct relation between amount of tree canopy as indexed by DIFN and moss cover. Postfire recovery of moss appeared to depend less on tree shade than on soil moisture and the micro-canopy afforded by herbaceous plants and litter. Shade, moisture, and soil temperature appeared to interact in early spring. Although shaded plots retained moisture on the soil surface longer than those plots exposed to greater solar irradiance, from February through April (when moisture was not limiting) their maximum soil temperatures were lower, which may have slowed seed germination and growth (e.g., max soil temperatures of Plots 2 and 18 in figure 4).

Seedling emergence, growth, and survival—

On February 10, 2005, the mean air temperature from 1000 to 1500 hours was 8 $^\circ$C (46 $^\circ$F), and soil temperatures at rooting level ranged from -2.0 to 0.5 $^\circ$C (28.4 to 32.9 $^\circ$F). Because the test plants are vernal species, we expected early seed germination; nevertheless, we were surprised that seeds of 10 of the 18 species had already germinated despite snow covering some of the plots. Mean emergence of four grass species, *Elymus elymoides, Festuca idahoensis, Poa secunda,* and *Pseudoroegnaria spicata,* in February was 45.0 percent. Leaves of these grasses averaged about 4 cm in length indicating seeds had germinated in the fall. Seeds of the grasses *P. secunda, E. elymoides* and *P. spicata* have been described as nondormant (Beckstead et al. 1995, Darris 2007). Goodwin et al. (1995) noted that seeds of *F. idahoensis* could be partially dormant as some germinated in fall and some in spring. Seeds of *Achnatherum thurberianum,* however, were apparently dormant when sown, as there was no visible emergence until mid March.

In February, emergence also was evident by the appearance of cotyledons of six forb species, *Balsamorhiza careyana, Calochortus macrocarpus, Erigeron filifolius, Eriogonum umbellatum, Lomatium triternatum* and *Zigadenus venenosus.* In early March, we observed the emergence of *Eriophyllum lanatum, Linum lewisii, Olsynium douglasii, Penstemon humilis,* and *Silene oreganum,* and in early April, the emergence of *Apocynum androsaemifolium* and *Lotus crassifolius.* Mean percentage germination of the 18 species collectively was 36.9 percent; of the 5 grasses, 46.3 percent; and 13 forbs, 33.3 percent. Mean germination of the lilioid monocots (*C. macrocarpus, O. douglasii,* and *Z. venenosus)* was 47.9 percent (table 5). The field germination of *B. careyana, L. lewisii,* and *L. triternatum* were much higher than their in vitro germination tests, confirming that the ex situ stratification and germination environment including light and temperature did not provide optimal germination conditions for these species. The germination of *A. androsaemifolium* was very low (2.5 percent) and no survivors were found in 2006. The germination of *E. filifolius* and *P. humilis* in 2006 was also low (< 20 percent).

Seedling survival as a percentage of seeds sown, calculated for each field visit, indicated that by late May, recruitment had virtually ceased while attrition increased. The mean survival of all species combined was 26.9 percent in April 2005, declined to 20.3 percent in June, and continued declining to 13.3 percent in May 2006 or half of the survival rate in April 2005. The mean survival calculated for each species tested for differences between years with a paired t-test (N = 20) was significantly lower in 2006 than 2005 (P < 0.05) with the exception

Table 5—Germination rate based on max germination from February through April 2005 and percentage of survival and cover in 2005 and 2006 of 18 native species from seeds sown in fall 2004 within the Eyerly Fire boundary on Green Ridge

Species	Germination		Survival		Cover		Height	
	Mean	(± sd)	2005	2006	2005	2006	2005	2006
	— — — — — — — — — Percent — — — — — — — — — —						Centimeters	
Grasses:								
Achnatherum thurberianum	32.8	18.3	29.0	13.4*	4.6	1.6*	6.0	7.1
Elymus elymoides	62.8	3.1	46.2	15.3*	12.6	12.9	6.9	9.2
Festuca idahoensis	48.1	19.2	30.5	9.5*	9.0	11.4	5.0	7.2
Poa secunda	46.3	19.7	26.1	15.8*	6.2	5.8	2.2	3.7*
Pseudoroegnaria spicata	41.6	11.9	25.8	5.7*	4.7	3.9	8.2	8.3
Forbs:								
Apocynum androsaemifolium	2.5	5.7	1.2	0.0*	0.0	0.0	<1	0.0
Balsamorhiza careyana	55.8	6.7	45.2	34.7*	14.9	17.9	4.8	6.5
Calochortus macrocarpus	54.7	14.0	37.0	24.7*	2.1	1.1	NA	6.0
Erigeron filifolius	11.0	12.0	1.4	1.2	0.1	0.4	<1	<1
Eriogonum umbellatum	34.5	19.9	21.6	11.3*	3.1	7.4	<1	2.3
Eriophyllum lanatum	16.9	11.2	13.9	5.9*	6.8	6.1	<1	3.1
Linum lewisii	34.3	14.6	29.4	25.8	4.4	12.7	3.1	8.0
Lomatium triternatum	70.8	21.6	45.1	35.8*	5.6	6.1	5.8	10.1*
Lotus crassifolius	22.4	11.9	21.7	1.1*	5.5	0.4*	1.8	2.3
Olsynium douglasii	45.0	17.2	29.8	22.3	4.2	1.8*	NA	6.2
Penstemon humilis	18.3	15.3	10.6	0.8*	0.5	0.2	<1	<1
Silene douglasii	23.1	14.9	12.7	4.1*	2.2	1.1	<1	2.7
Zigadenus venenosus	44.2	18.4	32.7	25.6*	3.8	2.4	NA	5.8

Note: Mean height of grasses and forbs were calculated from measurements of five sampled individuals, or all individuals if five or fewer were in plot. Significant difference between years shown with an asterisk (*) (p < 0.05) N = 20.

of *E. filifolius,* which had extremely low survival in 2005, and *L. lewisii,* which recruited new seedlings in 2006 (table 5). For each species, the trend in percentage of surviving seedlings from February through May is shown graphically in the appendix.

Generally, those species with a high percentage of germination had proportionally greater survival than those with low germination. The combination of germination and survival may be a good indicator of reproductive fitness in this environment. The percentage germination of *Balsamorhiza careyana, Calochortus macrocarpus, Linum lewisii, Lomatium triternatum, Olsynium douglasii*, and *Zigadenus venenosus* was higher than 33.3 percent (mean for all forbs), and their mean survival rate in 2006 was greater than 20 percent. In addition, the presence of *B. careyana, L. lewisii,* and *Z. venenosus* in 2006 on all plots including plot 2, the harshest plot that supported the least herbaceous cover, suggests that seedlings of these species' fitness includes being broadly adapted to a range of conditions at the Green Ridge site. It should be noted, however, that even if percentages of germination appear low, in the wild, the implications for judging seeding success are different than in an agricultural setting. A rate of 20 percent emergence for 50 seeds sown in > $1/16^{th}$ of a 1-m^2 plot represents potential for 10 individual plants to grow in that space. For a large, long-lived herb like *B. careyana* that would be an excessive density.

Measuring survival may be confounded by differences in dormancy of seeds of species adapted to the variable environment of a transitional forest/steppe interface. For example, we observed in 2006 a new cohort of *L. lewisii* seedlings. These seedlings averaged about four per plot and increased survival of *L. lewisii* from 20.3 percent to 25.8 percent. This carryover of seed viability and dormancy of this species is not unique to the Green Ridge site as it was previously reported for *L. lewisii* accessions at different elevations in Utah (Meyer and Kitchen 1994.)

Invertebrate herbivory of the germinants was first apparent in March 2005 when cotyledons were expanding. The species that most commonly had visible signs of herbivory during the cotyledon stage in March were *E. umbellatum,* *B. careyana,* and *L. triternatum.* In April, signs of herbivory were also visible on *L. lewisii, S. douglasii,* and *L. crassifolius* cotyledons. Insect predation of *L. crassifolius* was particularly severe in damaging cotyledons, shoots, and emerging leaves (fig. 3E), resulting in a major decrease in survival and cover between 2005 and 2006 (table 5). The overall rate of emergence was about 30 percent in mid March with much of the early mortality from frost heaving. The grass seedlings in plot 2 with little vegetation and high solar exposure died from desiccation and lethal temperatures because many of the seeds were displaced to the soil surface (figs. 3C, 4A). This may be because of the horizontal placement of the seeds that are normally "drilled" vertically into the soil when they disperse naturally with awns intact. The decline in survival from April through June 2005 appeared generally attributable to high soil surface temperatures, herbivory, and competition by annual exotic grasses. Because of episodic rainstorms through May 2005, moisture was retained in the soil-plant interface on the more vegetated plots resulting in the appearance of a botrytis-like mold on some of the seedlings detected only in one visit in early April.

By early April 2005, the dicotyledonous forbs were growing stems and true leaves. Additional leaves of the lilioid monocots (*C. macrocarpa, O. douglasii, Z. venenosus*) elongated in the following months of the growing season. By late May, leaf growth of the three species had slowed or stopped, and by June 2005, the leaves of many individuals had begun senescing particularly on the more exposed plots. Although most of the plants remained vegetative and immature in 2006, leaf growth of forbs continued (table 5). A proportion of *L. lewisii* (20 percent), *L. triternatum* (10 percent), and *E. lanatum* (10 percent) produced stems bearing buds and flowers indicating that they had grown to maturity within 2 years. Although the leaves of all the monocots increased in length between 2005 and 2006, none of them had grown to maturity or acquired enough resources to develop a flowering stem. Growth of dicot species also resulted in increasing cover. *Eriophylum lanatum* grew little in height but increased in lateral spread (table 5).

In February 2005, the leaves of the fall-emergent grasses *E. elymoides, F. idahoensis, P. spicata,* and *P. secunda* had lengthened to about 2 to 4 cm (0.8 to 1.6 in) (fig. 5). The leaves of *A. thurberianum* did not emerge until after February. However, leaf growth was rapid so that by May, mean leaf length was 6 cm. During the same period, leaves of *P. secunda* grew very little. Leaves grew in length between 2005 and 2006, but by the end of the second growing season, mean leaf length of *P. secunda,* a short-tufted grass, was 3.7 cm, or less than half the mean length of the four other grasses (fig. 5, table 5). Maturation apparently takes several years, as leaves were all basal and no grasses had developed flowering shoots. In 2006, the leaves of the grasses continued to increase in length, but the plants also increased biomass by sprouting new shoots (tillering). Cover of *A. thurberianum* was significantly lower in 2006 than in 2005, whereas the cover of the other grasses was not significantly different between the two years (table 5). The cover data however do not show the real increase in biomass and cover of the individual plants because the same amount of cover in 2006 was produced by significantly fewer surviving seedlings (table 5).

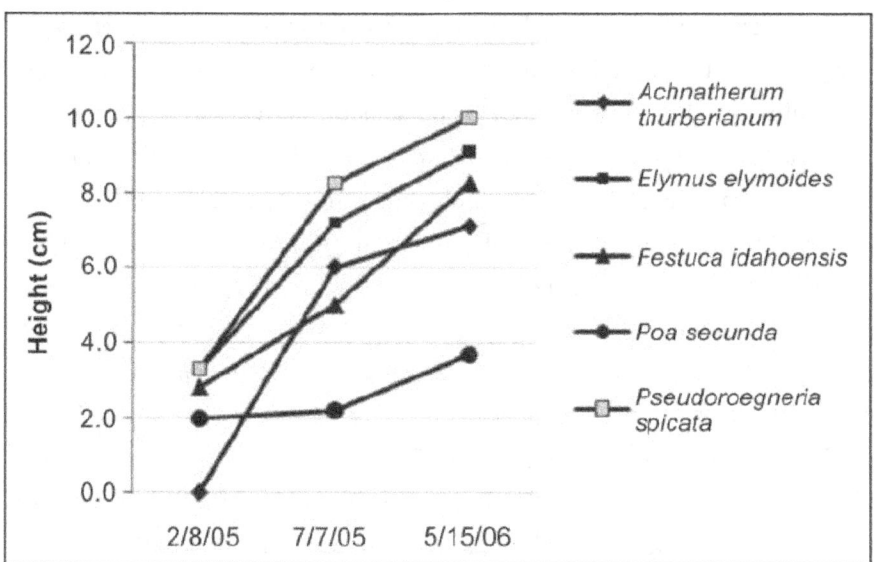

Figure 5—Mean leaf length of five native grass species over the first two growing seasons. Seeds were sown in late September 2004 in twenty 1-m^2 plots at the Green Ridge site in the east-side central Oregon Cascade Range.

The amount of aerial spread is what determines cover but does not really indicate fully the growth or level of occupancy of the plant. Forbs are a heterogeneous mixture of growth forms having both vertical and horizontal components of occupancy including that which takes place below ground. Above the ground, occupancy may expand by a plant's having vertically and horizontally spreading leaves, or a branching growth form, as for example, *B. careyana* and *L. lewisii*, respectively. Others grow primarily vertically with one elongating stem and slender leaves like *L. triternatum* or with usually two slender leaves that elongate like the lilioid monocots *C. macrocarpus*, *O. douglasii*, and *Z. venenosus*. For these species, cover is proportionally low relative to biomass. In contrast, vegetative spread by branching and horizontal growth is best represented by *E. lanatum*, which increased in cover from 3.1 percent to 7.4 percent between 2005 and 2006 although the percentage of survivors declined from 13.9 to 5.9 during the same period (table 5). This mixture of growth forms for a suite of herbs that all grow and flower during the same months is one way in which species optimize the vertical and horizontal space that they share.

Vegetative dynamics—
In 2006, the mean herbaceous cover of the 20 plots was 17.6 percent. Despite a decrease in survival of 46 percent, the mean cover of the 18 study species considered collectively on the 20 plots did not change significantly from 2005 to 2006 (5.0 and 5.1, respectively). The study species made up 29 percent of the herbaceous cover,

and the nonnative grasses having a mean cover of 5.4 percent composed 31 percent. However, in plots where annual, nonnative grasses were most dense and contributed more than 75 percent of the herbaceous cover, sown native species contributed less than 8 percent. The relative cover of the study species was negatively related to invasive cover (r^2 = 0.77, p < 0.001) in an exponential model, suggesting that the density of the annual nonnative grasses interfered significantly with the growth and spread of the study species (fig. 6).

Between 2004 and 2006, the invasive annual grass, *Bromus tectorum,* increased in abundance throughout the burned site where the 20-plot transect was located (fig. 3F). Although *B. tectorum* may have germinated in the fall, we did not detect emergence of *B. tectorum* until early March. *Bromus tectorum* commonly germinates in early spring when soils have high moisture content and are warmed (Martens et al. 1994, Roundy et al. 2007). Patches of *Vulpia myuros* (L.) C.C. Gmel., a nonnative grass that increases after fire (Howard 2006), also appeared in or near the plots. Although competition for resources by established native perennial species may inhibit *B. tectorum* (Chambers et al. 2007), under other conditions of disturbance, *B. tectorum* can outcompete native perennial species newly emergent from seed and inhibit their growth and survival (Goodwin et al. 1999). An ocular survey provided evidence of its spread: in 2004, *B. tectorum* was present < 10 m from 15 plots, present < 2 m from 13 plots, and inside 4 plots. In 2005, *B. tectorum* was identified inside 7 plots and in 2006, inside 13 plots. This study was not designed to examine

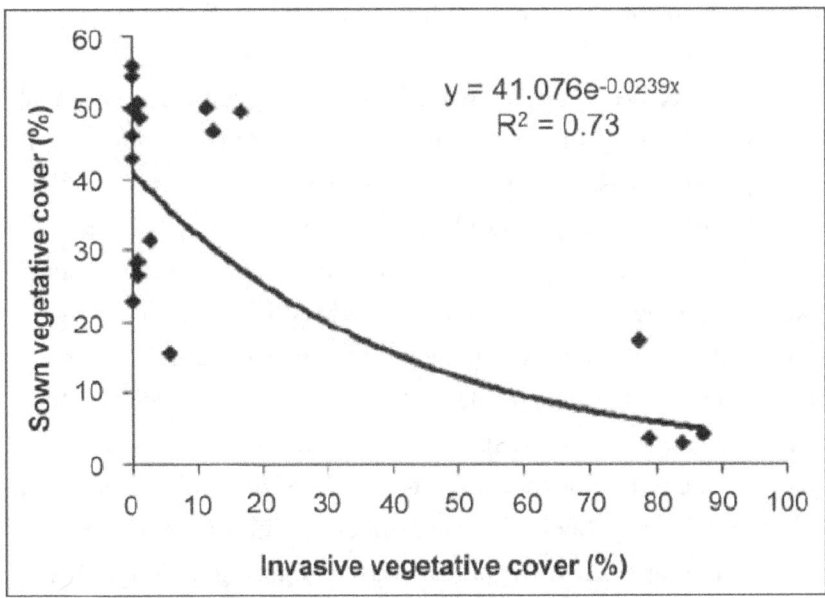

$$y = 41.076e^{-0.0239x}$$
$$R^2 = 0.73$$

Figure 6—Relation of the mean cover of invasive, nonnative grasses to the mean cover of native grasses and forbs in the second year of growth. Seeds were sown in late September 2004 in twenty 1-m^2 plots at the Green Ridge site in the east-side central Oregon Cascade Range.

competition effects. However, it appeared that survival and growth of sown species were not measurably affected when the density or cover of the nonnative grasses was low. This may be because invaders at first fill empty microsites (Tilman 1997). But if nonnative grasses reach a critical density or cover, the ability to establish native species from seed may be reduced (Beyers 2004, Forcella and Harvey 1983, Goodwin et al. 1999, Roundy et al. 2007).

Summary and Conclusions

Most of the sown species emerged early and established to some degree on most of the plots. Frost heaving in early spring, high soil surface temperatures, insect preda-tion, and the high density of invasive grasses appeared to be important microenvi-ronmental factors that affected survival and growth rates. Some juvenile forb and most grass species increased vegetative cover through clonal spread, a secondary mechanism for their propagation and persistence (Liston et al. 2003). However, if invasive grasses became dense in the immediate vicinity of the emergent seeds, the rate of seedling growth and survival was reduced (Roundy et al. 2007, Young and Evans 1978). Most of the native species in this study are long-lived perennials that take several years to reach maturity and, thus, are vulnerable to extirpation before they reproduce. Sowing seeds in the fall capitalizes on the vernal growth habit of the native species and allows the seedlings' maximum use of available moisture and nutrients for root and shoot growth. A secondary benefit might be increased com-petitiveness with annual nonnative grasses for limited resources (Beckstead et al. 1995; Goodwin et al. 1995, 1996).

Although traditional seed testing can yield information about a seed's potential performance (USDA FS 2008), field seed germination tests based on accumulated emergence over the growing season can be used to build a database of information that would increase the predictability of survival and establishment of species under a range of conditions. Field tests have the added benefit of producing information on some of the key environmental and biological conditions that influence early survival and growth. The in situ seed germination evaluations increased our under-standing of how environmental factors influence healthy germinating seed in the field. Unfortunately, because most of the species in this study did not reach matu-rity within the 2 years of observation, no inferences could be made about long-term establishment. To determine whether seeding can effectively introduce or accelerate the return of desired native species on degraded lands, monitoring for longer than 2 to 3 years is essential.

Dormancy may vary among seeds collected from a single location, which results in not all seeds germinating in the fall or spring (Goodwin et al. 1996,

Meyer and Kitchen 1994) and suggests an adaptation of these species to the highly variable temperature and moisture patterns on the east-side central Oregon Cascade Range. The evidence that seeds from a single source and species germinated at various times suggests that conditional dormancy and germination phenology of the grasses, the forb *Linum lewisii*, and possibly other species such as *Penstemon humilis* from this zone vary and should be examined further (Baskin and Baskin 1988, Meyer and Kitchen 1994, Meyer et al.1995). In addition to recognizing that there is variability within populations of critical seed traits such as dormancy and germination vigor, knowing the range in expression of those traits across the landscape will improve operational sowing strategies for seeds used in restoration or rehabilitation (Baskin and Baskin 1988, Meyer et al. 1995).

Flowering herbs endemic to the dry transition forests of the east-side Cascades have a long evolutionary history of adaptation and fitness in ecosystems noted for disturbance. Not only an attractive part of the landscape, they contribute to nutrient cycling, energy flow, wildlife nutrition, and the support of diverse, beneficial insects (Brown and Amacher 1999). Biodiversity is usually assessed in the context of genetic variation, species diversity, and ecosystem complexity that occurs in a unit of space (Brown 2000, Erickson et al. 2004). However, the functionally diverse flora of a plant community suggests differences in how space is occupied, a key consideration when rehabilitating a landscape (Pillar 1999, Tilman 1997). For example, the diversity of the 18 vernal species used in this study includes the differences in functional traits and characteristics of monocots and dicots as well as differences among species in seed-germination phenology, seedling maturation and growth, growth form, and root and leaf morphology (Baskin and Baskin 1988). Within the larger climatic and topographic sphere of influences, each species has evolved adaptive traits to function best (e.g., use limited resources) in its own microenvironment so that through natural selection and stochastic processes, the plant community may evolve toward optimal use of space and time (Pillar 1999, Tilman 1994). In the context of landscape rehabilitation or enhancement, the range of adaptability of any one species is not as effective in the long term as the aggregate range of adaptability of all its community members. However, the invasion of species following major or chronic disturbances disrupts the microniche function of the endemic species, particularly in semiarid systems. Invasions, unfortunately, are becoming more widespread, which increases the challenge of reestablishing the functionality of the native herbaceous flora while attempting to rehabilitate degraded landscapes (Chambers et al. 2007, Merriam et al. 2006, Monsen and Stevens 2004, Whisenant 1999).

For each of the 18 species, information based on this study, published literature, and other documents may be found in appendix 2.

Glossary

achene—A dry indehiscent, one-seeded fruit, formed from a single carpel and with the seed distinct from the fruit wall.

anthesis—The duration of life of a flower from bud opening, to fruit set.

apomictic/apogamy—Production of viable seed without sexual union (double fertilization).

awn—A long, bristle or thread-like outgrowth on glumes or lemmas found on tall grass species.

bolting—Rapid plant growth that goes from producing mostly leaves to producing mostly flowers and seeds.

caespitose—In tufts.

calyx—The whorl of sepals that collectively form the outer layer of the flower.

campanulate—Bell-shaped.

capitulum—The composite flower or seed head of members of the Asteraceae family.

carpel—The fertile female organ comprising the floral whorl known as the gynoecium of an angiosperm. Carpels may occur separately within the whorl or fuse together forming a compound structure (the pistil).

caryopsis—Fruit of grasses in which the coat (testa) of the single seed is indistinct from the interconnective fruit wall.

caudex—A trunk or stock

coleoptile—A leafy sheath that covers the emergent shoot of a germinating grass seed in the family Poaceae.

colluvium—The soil accumulated at the foot of slopes.

cordate—Heart shaped.

corolla—A collective term for the whorl, or whorls of petals in a flower.

cotyledon—An embryonic leaf formed from the embryo of an angiosperm or gymnosperm, and usually the first to appear upon germination. Monocotyledons typically have a single cotyledon; dicotyledons, two; and gymnosperms, several.

culm—The jointed and usually flowering secondary stem of a grass or sedge.

cymose—Having an inflorescence that is headed by a terminal flower bud followed by lateral flowers.

dehisce—Open spontaneously along proscribed sutures to release pollen, spores, or seeds.

depauperate—Lacking species abundance normally found elsewhere.

epigeal—When seeds germinate, the cotyledons appear above ground.

filiform—Like a thread.

follicle—A many-seeded dry fruit derived from a single carpel that splits longitudinally down one side at dehiscence.

glabrous—Hairless.

glume—Dry bract enclosing a grass spikelet.

hypogeal—When seeds germinate, the cotyledons remain below ground while the epicotyls elongate.

hypogynous ovary—Petals and sepals of flower attached at base of carpel or ovary.

in vitro—Outside a natural environment, usually in a laboratory.

inflorescence—The arrangement of flowers on a flowering stalk such as a raceme, spike, or cyme, without interruption by true, foliage leaves.

infructescence—Fruits formed of flowers making up an inflorescence.

involucre—A ring or cup of bracts (leaflike structures) that surround flowers under the capitulum (Asteraceae) or an umbel (Apiaceae).

lemma—Outer bract of a grass floret.

ligule—Membrane at junction of leaf base of grasses.

nectary—Modified plant tissue that secretes nectar.

outcross—The union of genes (cross fertilization) from one genetically distinct member of a species with another genetically distinct member.

papillate—Having papillae (small hair-like protuberances).

pappus—A ring of feathery hairs around fruit that act like a parachute; common in the Asteraceae family.

pedicel—The stalk of a flower in an inflorescence.

perianth—The floral envelope, calyx (sepals) or corolla (petals), or both.

pericarp—Part of fruit enclosing seeds.

pls—Pure live seed.

pollinator limited—Reduced fruit or seed set in a population or species owing to inadequate visitation by known pollen vectors (pollinators).

polyploidy—Having more than the usual two sets of chromosomes.

pubescence—Fuzz-like fine hairs on plant structures such as stems.

raceme—Inflorescence in which main axis bears flowers that bloom in succession toward the terminal.

rachis—Axis of pinnately compound leaf to which leaves are attached.

rhizome—A root-like stem lying horizontally on or under ground producing the buds of aerial (secondary) stems and bearing adventitious roots.

rhizomatous—Having rhizomes.

ruderal—Plant that readily grows in disturbed sites (waste places).

rugose—Wrinkled.

scabrous—Warty or with bumps.

scarification—Abrasion or other treatment to soften a hard seed coat of a dormant seed.

senescent—State of decline, dying.

sessile—Attachment on an organ to a stem without a connecting stalk. A sessile leaf lacks a petiole and a sessile flower lacks a pedicel.

spikelet—In grasses, a unit of the inflorescence in which a known cluster of flowers are subtended by the same pair of glumes.

staminode—Highly modified stamen.

stratification—Removal of seed dormancy through moisture and period of time in cold temperature.

tepals—Perianth organs in which true sepals or petals are anatomically indistinguishable.

ternate—Compound leaf having three leaflets.

tiller—In grasses, a new shoot arising upward from an adventitious bud at or near the base of the original shoot.

umbel—Inflorescence composed of flowers on stalks arising at same point resembling a flower head.

Sources: Hickey and King 2000, Porter 2008, Usher 1966.

Acknowledgments

Many thanks go to Andrew Neill for his fine technical support and careful management of seeds, field and lab crews, and data and to Dan Mikowski for his expertise and time in laying out the study in the field. I also appreciate all the technical help and labor that was contributed to this study, especially by Lynn Larson, Emmalie Goodwin, and Zak Weinstein. Al Chase, volunteer, provided important help in the field in locating species in sufficient abundance for seed collecting. Thanks also to the staff at Lucky Peak Nursery for carrying out the growout study and collecting the data. I also thank Nancy Leeper for her editing expertise, Peter Bernhardt for lending his botanical expertise, and Bill Stein for his careful, thoughtful, and thorough review. The study was funded in part by the Native Plant Program NFN3 from the USDA Forest Service.

English Equivalents

When you know:	Multiply by:	To find:
Millimeters (mm)	0.0394	Inches (in)
Centimeters (cm)	0.394	Inches
Meters (m)	3.281	Feet (ft)
Meters	1.094	Yards (yd)
Kilometers	.621	Miles
Square meters (m^2)	1.196	Square yards (yd^2)
Square kilometers	.386	Square miles
Hectares (ha)	2.471	Acres (ac)
Grams (g)	0.0022	Pounds (lb)
Kilograms (kg)	0.205	Pounds
Kilograms per hectare (kg/ha)	0.893	Pounds per acre (lb/ac)
Liters (L)	1.057	Quarts
Celsius (°C)	1.8 (+ 32)	Fahrenheit (°F)
Pure live seeds per square meter	.093	Pure live seeds per square foot (pls/ft^2)

Literature Cited

Agee, J.K. 1994. Fire and weather disturbances in terrestrial ecosystems of the eastern Cascades. Gen. Tech. Rep. PNW-GTR-320. Portland, OR: U.S. Department of Agriculture, Forest Service Pacific Northwest Research Station. 52 p.

Apfelbaum, S.I.; Bader, B.J.; Faessler, F.; Mahler, D. 1997. Obtaining and processing seeds. In: Packard, S.; Mutel, C.F., eds. The tallgrass restoration handbook for prairies, savannas, and woodlands. Washington, DC: Island Press: 99–126. Chapter 7.

Archer, A.J. 2000. *Achnatherum thurberianum.* In: Fire effects information system. Missoula, MT: U.S. Department of Agriculture, Forest Service, Rocky Mountain Research Station, Fire Sciences Laboratory. http://www.fs.fed.us/database/feis/. (October 4, 2006).

Archibald, C. 2006. Seed production protocols for *Anaphalis margaritacea, Eriophyllum lanatum* and *Eriogonum umbellatum.* Native Plants. (7) 1: 47–51.

Arno, S.F. 2000. Fire in western forest ecosystems. In: Brown, J.K.; Smith, J.K., eds. Wildland fire in ecosystems effects of fire on flora. Gen. Tech. Rep. RMRS-GTR-42-vol. 2. Ogden, UT: U.S. Department of Agriculture, Forest Service, Rocky Mountain Research Station: 97–120.

Association of Official Seed Analysts [AOSA]. 2003a. Handbook on seeds of browse-shrubs and forbs. Atlanta, GA: Browse-Shrub and Forb Committee, Association of Official Seed Analysts and U.S. Department of Agriculture, Forest Service, Southern Region. 246 p. http://www.nsl.fs.fed.us/Handbook%20on%20Seeds%20of%20Browse-Shrubs%20and%20Forbs.pdf. (December 2008).

Association of Official Seed Analysts [AOSA]. 2003b. Rules for testing seeds. Annapolis, MD: Rules committee of the Association of Official Seed Analysts. 166 p.

Barbour, J. 2002. Uses of the Westrup brush machine. In: Dumroese, R.K.; Riley, L.E.; Landis, T.D., technical coordinators. National proceedings: forest and conservation nursery associations—1999, 2000, and 2001. Proceedings RMRS-P-24. Ogden, UT: U.S. Department of Agriculture Forest Service, Rocky Mountain Research Station: 245–249.

Baskin, C.C.; Baskin, J.M. 1988. Germination ecophysiology of herbaceous plant species in a termperate region. American Journal of Botany. 75(2): 286–305.

Beckstead, J.; Meyer, S.E.; Allen, P.S. 1995. Effects of afterripening on cheatgrass (*Bromus tectorum*) and squirreltail (*Elymus elymoides*) germination. In: Roundy, B.A.; McArthur, E.D.; Haley, J.S.; Mard, D.K., eds. Proceedings: wildland shrub and arid land restoration symposium. Gen. Tech. Rep. INT-GTR-315. Ogden, UT: U.S. Department of Agriculture, Forest Service, Intermountain Research Station: 165–172.

Beyers, J.L. 2004. Postfire seeding for erosion control: effectiveness and impacts on native plant communities. Conservation Biology. 18(4): 947–956.

Brown, C.S.; Rice, K.J. 2000. The mark of Zorro: effects of the exotic annual grass *Vulpia myuros* on California native perennial grasses. Restoration Ecology. 8(1): 10–17.

Brown, J.K. 2000. Ecological principles, shifting fire regimes and management considerations. In: Brown, J.K.; Smith, J.K., eds. Wildland fire in ecosystems effects of fire on flora. Gen. Tech. Rep. RMRS-GTR-42-vol. 2. Ogden, UT: U.S. Department of Agriculture, Forest Service, Rocky Mountain Research Station: 185–203.

Brown, R.W.; Amacher, M.C. 1999. Selecting plant species for ecological restoration: a perspective for land managers. Revegetation with native species, proceedings 1997 Society for Ecological Restoration annual meeting. RMRS-P-8. Ogden, UT: U.S. Department of Agriculture, Forest Service, Rocky Mountain Research Station: 1–16.

Burgett, D.M.; Stringer, B.A.; Johnston, L.D. 1989. Nectar and pollen plants of Oregon and the Pacific Northwest. Blodgett, OR: Honeystone Press. 151 p.

Burton, P.J.; Burton, C.M. 2002. Promoting genetic diversity in the production of large quantities of native plant seed. Ecological Restoration 20. (2): 117–123.

Cane, J. 2005. Pollination needs of arrowleaf balsamroot, *Balsamorhiza sagittata* (Heliantheae: Ateraceae). Western North American Naturalist. 65(3): 359–364.

Cane, J.; Weber, M.; Yost, M.; Gardner, D. 2004. Alkaloids and old lace: pollen toxins exclude generalist pollinators from death camas (*Toxicoscordion* [= *Zigadenus*] *paniculatum)* (Melanthiaceae). [Abstract]. Salt Lake City, UT. http://www.2004.botanyconference.org/engine/search/index. php?func=detail&aid=1128. (January 2009).

Cavers, P.B.; Steel, M.G. 1984. Patterns of change in seed weight over time on individual plants. American Naturalist. 124: 324–335.

Cavieres, L.A.; Arroyo, M.T.K. 2000. Seed germination response to cold stratification period and thermal regime in *Phacelia secunda* (Hydrophyllaceae). Plant Ecology. 149: 1–8.

Chambers, J.C.; Roundy, B.A.; Blank, R.R.; Meyer, S.E.; Whittaker, A. 2007. What makes Great Basin sagebrush ecosystems invasible by *Bromus tectorum*? Ecological Monographs. 77(1): 117–145.

Clinebell, R.R.; Bernhardt, P. 1998. The pollination ecology of five species of *Penstemon* (Scrophulariaceae) in the tallgrass prairie. Annals of the Missouri Botanical Garden. 85: 126–136.

Close, D.C.; Beadle, C.L.; Battaglia, M. 2004. Foliar anthocyanin accumulation may be a useful indicator of hardiness in eucalypt seedlings. Forest Ecology and Management. 198: 169–181.

Daehler, C.C. 2003. Performance comparisons of co-occurring native and alien invasive plants: implications for conservation and restoration. Annual Revue of Ecological Systematics. 34: 183–211.

Darris, D. 2007. Fact sheet pine bluegrass *Poa secunda* J. Presl. Corvallis, OR: U.S. Department Agriculture, Natural Resources and Conservation Service, Plant Materials Center. http://Plant-Materials.nrcs.usda.gov. (February 17, 2009).

Deering, R.H.; Young, T.P. 2006. Germination speeds of exotic annual and native perennial grasses in California and the potential benefits of seed priming for grassland restoration. Grasslands. 16(1): 13–17. http://ucdavis.edu/publications/2006Priming.pdf. (March 2009).

Doescher, P.; Miller, R.; Winward, A. 1985. Effects of moisture and temperature on germination of Idaho fescue. Journal of Range Management. 38: 317–320.

Douglas, J.; Grabowski J.; Keith, B. 1997. A comparison of seed cleaning techniques for improving quality of eastern gamagrass seed. Jackson, MS: U.S. Department of Agriculture, Natural Resource Conservation Service. Technical Note. 13(7): 43–47.

Drake, D.; Ewing, K.; Dunn, P. 1998. Germination of native plant seeds from the south Puget Sound prairies of Washington state. Restoration and Management Notes. 16(1): 33–40.

Durham, R.E.; Sackschewsky, M.R. 2004. W-519 Sagebrush mitigation project FY-2004 final review and status. Richland, WA: U.S. Department of Energy, Pacific Northwest National Laboratory. 88 p.

Ellison, R.L.; Thompson, J.N. 1987. Variation in seed and seedling size: the effects of seed herbivores on *Lomatium grayi* (Umbelliferae). Oikos 49: 269–280.

Erickson, V.J.; Mandel, N.L.; Sorensen, F.C. 2004. Landscape patterns of phenotypic variation and population structuring in a selfing grass, *Elymus glaucus* (blue wildrye). Canadian Journal of Botany. 82: 1776–1789.

Evans, R.A.; Young, J.A. 1978. Effectiveness of rehabilitation practices following wildfire in a degraded big sagebrush-downy brome community. Journal of Range Management. 31(3): 185–188.

Flessner, T.R.; Darris, D.C. 2001. Progress report of activities year 2000. Corvallis, OR: USDA Natural Resources Conservation Service Plant Materials Center. http://plant-materials.nrcs.usda.gov/pubs/orpmcra2000.pdf. (December 2008).

Forcella, F.; Harvey, S.J. 1983. Eurasian weed infestation in western Montana in relation to vegetation and disturbance. Madrono. 30: 102–109.

Franklin, J.F.; Dyrness, C.T. 1973. Natural vegetation of Oregon and Washington. Gen. Tech. Rep. PNW-8. Portland, OR: U.S. Department of Agriculture, Forest Service, Pacific Northwest Forest and Range Experiment Station. 417 p.

Gardenbed 2004. http://www.gardenbed.com. (August 15, 2006).

Gilky, H.M.; Dennis, L.R.J. 2001. Handbook of Northwestern plants. Corvallis, OR: Oregon State University Press. 494 p.

Goldblatt, P.; Manning, J.C. 2009. The iris family natural history and classification. Portland, OR: Timber Press, Inc. 336 p.

Goodwin, J.R.; Doescher, P.S.; Eddleman, L.E. 1995. After-ripening in *Festuca idahoensis* seeds: adaptive dormancy and implications for restoration. Restoration Ecology. 3(2): 137–142.

Goodwin, J.R.; Doescher, P.S.; Eddleman, L.E. 1996. Germination of Idaho fescue and cheatgrass seeds from coexisting populations. Northwest Science. 70(3): 230–241.

Goodwin, J.R.; Doescher, P.S.; Eddleman, L.E; Zobel, D.B. 1999. Persistence of Idaho fescue on degraded sagebrush steppe. Journal of Range Management. 52: 187–198.

Groen, A.H. 2005. *Apocynum androsaemifolium.* In: Fire Effects Information System. U.S. Department of Agriculture, Forest Service, Rocky Mountain Research Station, Fire Sciences Laboratory. http://www.fs.fed.us/database/feis/. (May 09, 2006).

Gundale, M.J.; Sutherland, S.; DeLuca, T.H. 2008. Fire, native species, and soil resource interactions influence the spatio-temporal invasion pattern of *Bromus tectorum*. Ecography. 31: 201–210.

Hardegree, S.P.; Jones, T.A.; VanVactor, S.S. 2002. Variability in thermal response of primed and non-primed seeds of squirreltail (*Elymus elymoides* (Raf.) Swezey and *Elymus multisetus* (J.G. Smith) M.E. Jones). Annals of Botany. 89: 311–319.

Harmond, J.E.; Brandenburg, N.R.; Klein, L.M. 1968. Mechanical seed cleaning and handling. U.S. Department of Agriculture. Agric. Handb. 354. Washington, D.C. 54 p.

Hassell, W.; Beavers, W.R.; Ouellette, S.; Mitchell, T., comps. 1996. Seeding rate statistics for native and introduced species [tables]. Washington, DC: U.S. Department of the Interior, National Park Service; U.S. Department of Agriculture, Natural Resources Conservation Service. 26 p.

Hickey, M.; King, C. 2000. The Cambridge illustrated glossary of botanical terms. Cambridge, New York: Cambridge University Press. 208 p.

Hitchcock, A.S. 1951. Manual of the grasses of the United States. 2nd ed. revised. New York: Dover Publishing, Inc. 569 p. Vol. 1.

Hitchcock, C.L; Cronquist, A. 1973. Flora of the Pacific Northwest. Seattle, WA: University of Washington Press. 730 p.

Howard, J.L. 1992. *Zigadenus venenosus*. In: Fire Effects Information System. U.S. Department of Agriculture, Forest Service, Rocky Mountain Research Station, Fire Sciences Laboratory. http://www.fs.fed.us/database/feis/. (October 4, 2006).

Howard, J.L. 1997. *Poa secunda*. In: Fire Effects Information System. U.S. Department of Agriculture, Forest Service, Rocky Mountain Research Station, Fire Sciences Laboratory. http://www.fs.fed.us/database/feis/. (October 4, 2006).

Howard, J.L. 2006. *Vulpia myuros*. In: Fire Effects Information System. U.S. Department of Agriculture, Forest Service, Rocky Mountain Research Station, Fire Sciences Laboratory. http://www.fs.fed.us/database/feis/. (December 4, 2008).

Iriondo, J.M.; Perez, C. 1999. Propagation from seeds and seed preservation. In: Bowes, B.G., ed. Plant propagation and conservation. New York: The New York Botanical Garden Press: 46–57.

Johnson, C.G. 1998. Vegetation response after wildfires in national forests of northeastern Oregon. R6-NR-ECOL-TP-06-98. Portland, OR: U.S. Department of Agriculture, Forest Service, Pacific Northwest Region. 128 p. + appendices.

Johnson, S.A.; Bruederle, L.P.; Tomback, D.F. 1998. A mating system conundrum: hybridization in *Apocynum* (Apocynaceae). American Journal of Botany. 85(9): 1316–1323.

Jones, T.A. 2006. Plant guide. Bottlebrush squirreltail and big squirreltail (*Elymus elymoides* (Raf.) Swezey and *Elymus multisetus* M.E. Jones). http://plants.usda. gov/plantguide/pdf/pg_elmu3.pdf. (July 2010).

Jorgensen, K.R.; Wilson, G.R. 2004. Seed germination. In: Monsen, S.B.; Stevens, R.; Shaw, N.L., comps. Restoring western ranges and wildlands. Gen. Tech. Rep. RMRS-GTR-136-vol-3. Fort Collins, CO: U.S. Department of Agriculture, Forest Service, Rocky Mountain Research Station: 723–732.

Kearns, C.A.; Inouye, D.W. 1994. Fly pollination of *Linum lewisii* (linaceae). American Journal of Botany. 81(9): 1091–1095.

Keeley, J.E. 2004. Ecological impacts of wheat seeding after a Sierra Nevada wildfire. International Journal of Wildland Fire. 13: 73–78.

Kephart, S.; Reynolds, R.J.; Rutter, M.T.; Fenster, C.B.; Dudash, M.R. 2006. Pollination and seed predation by moths on *Silene* and allied Caryophyllaceae: evaluating a model system to study the evolution of mutualisms. New Phytologist. 169: 667–680.

Kruckeberg, A.R. 1982. Gardening with native plants of the Pacific Northwest: an illustrated guide. Seattle, WA: University of Washington Press. 252 p.

Kruskal, W.H.; Wallis, W.A. 1952. Use of ranks in one-criterion variance analysis. Journal of the American Statistical Association. 47(260): 583–621.

Lambert, S. 2005. Guidebook to the seeds of native and non-native grasses, forbs and shrubs of the Great Basin. Tech. Bull. 2005-04. Boise, ID: U.S. Department of the Interior, Bureau of Land Management. 133 p.

Legler, B., contributor. 2006. Burke Museum of Natural History and Culture [Database]. Seattle, WA: University of Washington. http://biology.burke. washington.edu/herbarium/imagecollection.php?Genus=Olsynium&Species= douglasii. (December 2008).

Linhart, Y.B. 1995. Restoration, revegetation, and the importance of genetic and evolutionary perspectives. In: Roundy, B.A.; McArthur, E.D.; Haley, J.S.; Mard, D.K., eds. Proceedings: wildland shrub and arid land restoration symposium. Gen. Tech. Rep. INT-GTR-315. Ogden, UT: U.S. Department of Agriculture, Forest Service, Intermountain Research Station: 271–287.

Liston, A.; Wilson, B.L.; Robinson, W.A.; Doescher, P.S.; Harris, N.R.; Svejcar, T. 2003. The relative importance of sexual reproduction versus clonal spread in an aridland bunchgrass. Oecologia. 137: 216–225.

Lodewick, R.; Lodewick, K. 1999. Key to the genus *Penstemon*. Eugene, OR: 10th Ave. Press. 136 p.

Lofflin, D.L.; Kephart, S.R. 2005. Outbreeding, seedling establishment, and maladaptation in natural and reintroduced populations of rare and common *Silene douglasii* (Caryophyllaceae). American Journal of Botany. 92(10): 1691–1700.

Martens, E.; Palmquist, D.; Young, J.A. 1994. Temperature profiles for germination of cheatgrass versus native perennial bunchgrasses. In: Monsen, S.B.; Kitchen, S.G., comps. Proceedings—ecology and management of annual rangelands. Gen. Tech. Rep. INT-GTR-313. Ogden, UT: U.S. Department of Agriculture, Forest Service, Intermountain Research Station: 238–243.

McKown, R.; Kuroki, G.; Warren, G. 1996. Cold responses of *Arabidopsis* mutants impaired in freezing tolerance. Journal of Experimental Botany. 47: 1919–1925.

McWilliams, J. 2002. *Balsamorhiza sagittata*. In: Fire Effects Information System. U.S. Department of Agriculture, Forest Service, Rocky Mountain Research Station, Fire Sciences Laboratory. http://www.fs.fed.us/database/feis/. (October 4, 2006).

Merriam, K.E.; Keeley, J.E.; Beyers, J.L. 2006. Fuel breaks affect nonnative species abundance in Californian plant communities. Ecological Applications. 16(2): 515–527.

Meyer, S.E.; Kitchen, S.G. 1994. Life history variation in blue flax (*Linum perenne*: Linaceae): seed germination phenology. American Journal of Botany. 81(5): 528–535.

Meyer, S.E.; Kitchen, S.G.; Carlson, S.L. 1995. Seed germination timing patterns in intermountain *Penstemon* (Scrophulariaceae). American Journal of Botany. 82: 377–389.

Miller, H.C.; Clausnitzer, D.; Borman, M.M. 1999. Medusahead. In: Sheley, R.L.; Petroff, J.K., eds. Biology and management of noxious rangeland weeds. Corvallis, OR: Oregon State University Press. 438 p.

Miller, M.T.; Antos, J.A.; Allen, G.A. 2004. Dormancy and flowering in two mariposa lilies (*Calochortus*) with contrasting distribution patterns. Canadian Journal of Botany. 82: 1790–1799

Monsen, S.B.; Stevens, R. 2004. Seedbed preparation and seeding practices. In: Monsen, S.B.; Stevens, R.; Shaw, N.L., comps. Restoring western ranges and wildlands. Gen. Tech. Rep. RMRS-GTR-136-Vol 1. Fort Collins, CO: U.S. Department of Agriculture, Forest Service, Rocky Mountain Research Station: 121–154.

Mosely, J.C.; Bunting, S.C.; Monoukian, M.E. 1999. Cheatgrass. In: Sheley, R.L.; Petroff, J.K., eds. Biology and management of noxious rangeland weeds. Corvallis, OR: Oregon State University Press: 175–188.

O'Brien, M.H. 1980. The pollination biology of a pavement plain: pollinator visitation patterns. Oecologia. 47: 213–218.

Ogle, D.G. 2008. Plant Guide *Pseudoroegnaria spicata*. Boise, ID: U.S. Department of Agriculture, Natural Resources Conservation Service, Idaho State Office. http://Plant-Materials.nrce.usda.gov. (February 18, 2009).

Ollerton, J.; Lack, A. 1996. Partial predispersal seed predation in *Lotus corniculatus* L. (Fababceae) Seed Science Research. 6: 65–69.

Oregon Climate Service. 2009. Online climate data. Corvallis, OR: Oregon State University. http://www.ocs.oregonstate.edu. (February 16, 2009).

Parkinson, H., comp. 2003. Landscaping with native plants of the Intermountain Region. Tech. Ref. 1730-3. Boise, ID: U.S. Department of the Interior, Bureau of Land Management, Idaho State Office. 47 p.

Parkinson, H.; DeBolt, A. 2005a. Propagation protocol for production of container *Eriogonum umbellatum* Torr. plants. In: Native Plant Network. Moscow, ID: University of Idaho, College of Natural Resources, Forest Research Nursery. http://www.nativeplantnetwork.org. (February 17, 2009).

Parkinson, H.; DeBolt, A. 2005b. Propagation protocol for production of container *Lomatium triternatum* (Pursh.) Coult. & Rose. plants. In: Native Plant Network. Moscow, ID: University of Idaho, College of Natural Resources, Forest Research Nursery. http://www.nativeplantnetwork.org. (February 17, 2009).

Pendleton, R.L.; Kitchen, S.G.; Mudge, J.; McArthur, E.D. 2008. Origin of the flax cultivar "Appar" and its position within the *Linum perenne* complex. International Journal of Plant Sciences. 169(3): 445–453.

Peters, J., ed. 2000. Tetrazolium testing handbook. Contribution No. 29 to the Handbook on seed testing. Lincoln, NE: Association of Official Seed Analysts.

Pettersson, M.W. 1991. Flower herbivory and seed predation in *Silene vulgaris* (Caryophyllaceae): effects of pollination and phenology. Ecography. 14(1): 45–50.

Pillar, V.D. 1999. On the identification of optimal plant functional types. Journal of Vegetation Science. 10: 631–640.

Pojar, J.; Mackinnon, A., comps. 1994. Plants of the Pacific Northwest coast. Edmonton, AB: Lone Pine Publishing. 528 p.

Porter, C.L. 2008. Taxonomy of flowering plants. Caldwell NJ: The Blackburn Press. 488 p.

Reeves, S.L. 2006. *Linum lewisii.* In: Fire Effects Information System. U.S. Department of Agriculture, Forest Service, Rocky Mountain Research Station, Fire Sciences Laboratory. http://www.fs.fed.us/database/feis/. (March 21, 2007).

Robichaud, P.R.; Beyers, J.L.; Neary, D.G. 2000. Evaluating the effectiveness of postfire rehabilitation treatments. Gen. Tech. Rep. RMRS-GTR-63. Fort Collins, CO: U.S. Department of Agriculture, Forest Service, Rocky Mountain Research Station. 85 p.

Rose, R.; Chachulski, C.E.C; Haase, D.L. 1998. Propagation of Pacific Northwest native plants. Corvallis, OR: Oregon State University Press. 248 p.

Roundy, B.A.; Hardegree, S.P.; Chambers, J.C.; Whittaker, A. 2007. Prediction of cheatgrass field germination potential using wet thermal accumulation. Rangeland Ecology and Management. 60: 613–623.

Schoennagel, T.L.; Waller, D.M. 1999. Understory responses to fire and artificial seeding in an eastern Cascades *Abies grandis* forest, U.S.A. Canadian Journal of Forest Research. 29: 1393–1401.

Sheley, R.L.; Half, M.L. 2006. Enhancing native forb establishment and persistence using a rich seed mixture. Restoration Ecology. 14(4): 627–635.

Simonin, K.A. 2001. *Elymus elymoides.* In: Fire Effects Information System, U.S. Department of Agriculture, Forest Service, Rocky Mountain Research Station, Fire Sciences Laboratory. http://www.fs.fed.us/database/feis/. (October 4, 2006).

Simpson, M. 2007. Forested plant associations of the Oregon East Cascades. Tech. Pap. R6-NR-ECOL-TP-03-2007. Portland, OR: U.S. Department of Agriculture, Forest Service, Pacific Northwest Region. http://www.reo.gov/ecoshare/ Publications/documents/080702FS-MS_Forested_Plant_Assn_lores.pdf. (April 21, 2009).

Suna, H.; Van Campen, B. 2003. Eyerly Fire weed BAER monitoring report Sisters Ranger District. 6 p. Unpublished report. On file with: USDA Forest Service, Deschutes National Forest, Sisters Ranger District, P.O. Box 249, Sisters, OR 97759.

Tepedino, V.J. 2003. What's in a name? The confusing case of the death camas bee, *Andrena astragali* Viereck and Cockerell (Hymenoptera: Andrenidae). Journal of Kansas Entomological Society. 76(2): 194–197.

Thompson, J.N.; Pellmyr, O. 1989. Origins of variance in seed number and mass: interaction of sex expression and herbivory in *Lomatium salmoniflorum*. Oecologia. 79: 395–402.

Tilman, D. 1994. Competition and biodiversity in spatially structured habitats. Ecology. 75(1) 2–16.

Tilman, D. 1997. Community invasibility, recruitment limitation, and grassland biodiversity. Ecology. 78(1): 81–92.

Tyson, H. 1989. Genetic control of seed weight in flax (*Linum usitatissimum*) and possible implications. Theoretical and Applied Genetics. 77: 260–270.

U.S. Department of Agriculture, Forest Service [USDA FS]. 1937 [reprinted 1988]. Range plant handbook. Mineola, NY: Dover Publications. 816 p.

U.S. Department of Agriculture, Forest Service [USDA FS]. 2002. Eyerly Fire Burned-Area Report. Bend, OR: Deschutes and Ochoco National Forests, Crooked River National Grassland, Fire & Aviation. http://www.fs.fed.us/r6/ centraloregon/fires/2002/eyerly/baer.shtml. (December 2006).

U.S. Department of Agriculture, Forest Service [USDA FS]. 2004a. Burned-area emergency rehabilitation. FSM 2500, Ch. 2523. Amend. 2500–2004-1. Washington, DC.

U.S. Department of Agriculture, Forest Service [USDA FS]. 2004b. Final environmental impact statement Eyerly Fire Salvage Project. Sisters, OR: Sisters Ranger District, Deschutes National Forest. 604 p.

U.S. Department of Agriculture, Forest Service [USDA FS]. 2006a. Notice of Proposed Native Plant Material Policy, Forest Service Manual (FSM) 2070. Native Plants. Federal Register. 71(102): 30375-30376. http://www.nplnews.com/fedregister/2006/may262006-fs-plant-fsm2070.htm. (December 2008).

U.S. Department of Agriculture, Forest Service [USDA FS]. 2006b. Bend, OR: Bend Seed Extractory. http://www.nps.gov/plants/sos/bendcollections/index.htm. (January 2007).

U.S. Department of Agriculture, Forest Service [USDA FS]. 2008. Nursery manual for native plants: a guide for tribal nurseries. Vol 1. Nursery Management. Dumroese, R.K.; Luna, T.; Landis, T.D., eds. Agriculture Handbook 730.

U.S. Department of Agriculture, Natural Resources Conservation Service [USDA NRCS]. 2006. The PLANTS Database, version 3.5. Baton Rouge, LA: National Plant Data Center. http://plants.usda.gov. (October 23, 2008).

U.S. Department of the Interior Bureau of Land Management [USDI BLM]. 2003. Landscaping with native plants of the Intermountain Region. Tech. Ref. 1730-3. Boise, ID. 47 p.

Usher, G. 1966. The Wordsworth dictionary of botany. London: Constable and Co., Ltd. 404 p.

Valencia-Diaz, S.; Montaña, C. 2005. Temporal variability in the maternal environment and its effect on seed size and seed quality in *Flourensia cernua* DC. (Asteraceae). Journal of Arid Environments. 63: 686–695.

Vance, N.; Neill, A.; Morton, F. 2006. Native grass seeding and forb planting establishment. Native Plants Journal. 7(1): 35–46.

Whisenant, S.G. 1999. Repairing damaged wildlands a process-oriented, landscape-scale approach. Cambridge, United Kingdom: Cambridge University Press. 312 p.

Wickens, G.E. 1998. Ecophysiology of economic plants in arid and semi-arid lands. New York: Springer. 343 p.

Wilderman, D.L. 2003. Effects of wildfire on high-quality shrub-steppe vegetation, Cleveland Natural Area Preserve, south-central Washington state. The Phlox Phlyer—Newsletter of the Columbia Basin Chapter of the Washington Native Plant Society. 7(6): 1–2.

Wright, J.W.; Meagher, T.R. 2003. Pollination and seed predation drive flowering phenology in *Silene latifolia* (Caryophyllaceae). Ecology. 84(8): 2062–2073.

Young, J.A.; Evans, R.A. 1978. Population dynamics after wildfires in sagebrush grasslands. Journal of Range Management. 31(4): 283–289.

Young, J.A.; Evans, R.A. 1979. Arrowleaf balsamroot and mules ear seed germination. Journal of Range Management. 32(1): 71–74.

Young, J.A.; Young, C.G. 1986. Seeds of wildland plants. Portland, OR: Timber Press, Inc. 236 p.

Zlatnik, E. 1999. *Pseudoroegneria spicata*. In: Fire Effects Information System. U.S. Department of Agriculture, Forest Service, Rocky Mountain Research Station, Fire Sciences Laboratory. http://www.fs.fed.us/database/feis/. (October 4, 2006).

Zouhar, K.L. 2000. *Festuca idahoensis*. In: Fire Effects Information System. U.S. Department of Agriculture, Forest Service, Rocky Mountain Research Station, Fire Sciences Laboratory. http://www.fs.fed.us/database/feis/. (October 4, 2006).

Appendix 1: Growout Results at Lucky Peak Nursery

An important consideration when developing a seed collection program is to find local seed collection areas that will provide maximum number of viable seeds for the minimum expenditure of resources. Possible seed transfer issues can be circumvented by selecting areas as close as possible to the areas planned for treatment. However, this may present a constraint if these locations do not have enough plants to supply sufficient seed. When seed sources appear to be inadequate for supplying local seed, or seed collection in the wild becomes infeasible, nurseries that increase seed through cultivation may be used to supply seeds for rehabilitation and restoration (Archibald 2006). If seed transfer guidelines are not known, seeds for nursery production are often collected from parent plants distributed across an area thought to represent the range of conditions to which the species has adapted and where the seeds will be used. This strategy is used in part because small seed lots are costly and more difficult to manage. However, broad collections to bracket genetic adaptation in the long term may be costly as well if establishment rates are low (Burton and Burton 2002).

To determine the feasibility of increasing seeds collected from a restricted seed collection area < 26 km^2 (10 mi^2), seeds from native herbaceous species were collected at Green Ridge, on the Sisters Ranger District, Deschutes National Forest, during the summer of 2005. The cleaned seeds were brought to the Lucky Peak Nursery north of Boise, Idaho (Clarke Fleege, Nursery Manager, Lucky Peak Nursery, Boise National Forest). The seeds were sown in the fall of that year to test the efficacy of growing plants to maturity under nursery conditions to produce seed for future use by the district. Enough seeds of 11 species were available for sowing, including 4 grass and 7 forb species (table 6).

Of the 11 species grown from seed, only *Lomatium triternatum* and *Balsamorhiza careyana* did not reach maturity, flower, and produce seeds (table 6). These two, deep-rooted and long-lived species take several years to mature in the wild. The other species produced seeds that were collected once or twice over 3 years. The percentage of the yield in some cases exceeded 10,000 percent (table 6). *Silene douglasii* was notable for its high productivity in the nursery setting: from 0.08 lb of seed sown in 2005, the accumulated amount of seed produced from 2007 through 2008 was about 14 lb. This high rate of yield suggests that *S. douglasii* would be an excellent candidate for nursery growout. *Lotus crassifolius* also benefited from nursery conditions: from about 0.5 lb of seed, this species was able to produce 15 lb in 2 of the 3 years. Most of the species required 2 years to reach sufficient maturity

Table 6—Seed yield by weight and percentage of the growout seed production at Lucky Peak Nursery Boise, Idaho, from seeds of native forb and grass seeds collected at Green Ridge on the Deschutes National Forest, east-side central Oregon Cascades Range

Species	Sown seed	Harvest date		Yield				
		2007	2008	2006	2007	2008	Total	Increase
	Pounds			— — — — — — *Pounds* — — — — — —				*Percent*
Forbs:								
Balsamorhiza careyana	0.25	N.H.	N.H.					
Eriogonum umbellatum	0.20	N.H.	7/30		25.00	5.48	30.48	15,140
Eriophyllum lanatum	0.10	7/18	N.H.		32.00		32.00	31,900
Linum lewisii var. *lewisii*	0.10	6/28	N.H.	0.05	0.50		0.55	450
Lomatium triternatum	0.30	N.H.	N.H.					
Lotus crassifolius	0.40	N.H.	7/24			15.45	15.45	3,762
Silene douglasii	0.08	7/12	7/15		13.51	0.45	13.96	17,350
Grasses:								
Elemus elymoides	0.30	6/25	7/2	2.74	21.75	2.57	27.06	8,920
Festuca idahoensis	0.08	6/16	6/26		9.00	2.15	11.15	13,838
Poa secunda	0.05	6/20	7/2		8.50	4.46	12.96	25,820
Pseudoroegnaria spicata	0.25	6/20	7/2		3.50	0.81	4.31	1,624

N.H. = No harvest.

for seed production. The exceptions were *Elymus elymoides* and *Linum lewisii,* which produced a low amount of seed the first year.

The results of this growout trial demonstrate that nurseries can play an essential role for efficiently increasing the amount of seed of diverse species that would be needed for wide-scale seeding programs. Because 2 years is probably a minimum and may be optimum for most species to obtain high seed yield, postfire seeding would not be possible with this seed immediately after a burn. It is important that seed be collected and properly stored so it could become the basis of an ongoing seed bank program. Seeds of key native plant species collected from representative locations of a plant association and within an effective elevational range would then be made available in the event of fire or other disturbance that occurred in comparable locations.

Appendix 2: Summarized Information by Species

All taxonomic nomenclature follows USDA NRCS PLANTS Database, National Plant Data Center, Baton Rouge, LA 70874-4490 USA. (http://plants.usda.gov, 5 June 2009).

Apocynum androsaemifolium L.
Spreading dogbane
Apocynaceae
APAN2

Apocynum androsaemifolium L. is a rhizomatous, perennial herb with branching, erect stems 20–50 cm having opposite, somewhat drooping, ovate leaves. Stems and leaves have a milky sap. The inflorescence is cymose with campanulate or tubular flowers; the corolla is white to pink with pink veins, 5–10 mm; filaments of stamens curved so that anthers converge over stigma, pistil surrounded at base by five nectaries; fruit are long, narrow follicles that turn from green to pinkish brown when mature; tapering cylindrical seeds have attached, tufted hairs.

Distribution and habitat

Range is from Alaska and Canada south throughout most of the United States except for the Southeast. It has a broad distribution across a range of environments, plant community types, and elevations (50–2000 m) on dry hillsides, riparian zones, valleys, and foothills, to semialpine slopes. Grows in open woods, meadows, along woodland edges and roadsides, and in disturbed openings such as powerline rights-of-way; an early seral species but also tolerates shade. *Apocynum androsaemifolium* is fire adapted with deep rhizomes that regenerate after wildfire.

Reproductive ecology

Apocynum androsaemifolium is self-incompatible, and therefore, relies on sexual reproduction through insect vectors to reproduce. However, it appears to persist primarily through rhizomatous propagules to the extent that a colony of *A. androsaemifolium* might be a clone. The species has a long flowering interval, which for the east-side central Oregon Cascade Range may be from June through August. Although the plant is reportedly toxic to livestock, the flowers produce nectar that attracts and helps to support a wide variety of insects important to the pollination of associated plants. *Apocynum androsaemifolium* also has been described as "keystone prey" for insects. About 71 species have been recorded visiting the flowers including bees, wasps, flies, butterflies, and moths. Although most insects appear to visit the flowers for nectar, few have been found carrying *A. androsaemifolium* pollen, and the effective pollinator has not been identified. The reported fruit-to-flower ratio is low, or < 2 percent and seed set is poor; however, the

filled-seed rate of seeds collected at Green Ridge in the east-side Oregon Cascade Range was 53.8 percent in 2004. Seeds have hairs and are wind dispersed.

Propagation

Seeds mature from mid September through early October. Because this species is so clonal in its propagation, care should be taken to collect seeds from colonies that are distinctly separated from each other to ensure genetic diversity in the seed mix. Mature fruits are harvested by hand from mid through late September at Green Ridge. The long, narrow follicles are collected just before they split but when as dry as possible, placed in paper bags, and returned to the lab to dry further. After a few days to a week when they are dry and brittle and split easily, seeds are removed. Seeds are light brown when they are mature; dark brown seeds are usually empty. The tufted hairs detach readily from the seeds and tend to float in the air. Seeds can easily be cleaned with screens. Of fresh seeds from Green Ridge that dried 2 weeks in the lab, the number per kilogram was 2,684,700. The seeds store well, but seeds require cold stratification (1–4 °C) before sowing. Viability can be low; seeds tetrazolium (TZ) tested from the Puget Sound lowland prairie had 10-percent viability, and germination with 12 weeks stratification was 2 percent. Filled seed was 54 percent and seed viability of the Green Ridge seeds by tetrazolium testing was 55 percent. The germination rate on seeds stratified for 10 weeks was 28.0 percent with 74.8 percent of the seeds moldy. Low seed viability and poor germination may be due to self pollination or lack of maturity. The study seeds sown at Green Ridge in late September germinated poorly (< 2 percent). The trend in emergence and survival peaks in early May as shown in figure A1. There were virtually no survivors the following year. *Apocynum androsaemifolium* is reportedly difficult to grow in poor-quality soil, but grows well under greenhouse conditions and once established, under the right conditions, can become weedy. We observed plants resprouting from live root crowns or rhizomes below the soil surface 2 years after a wildfire at Green Ridge. In areas where this species is part of the prefire community, propagation by planting rather than seeding may result in better establishment.

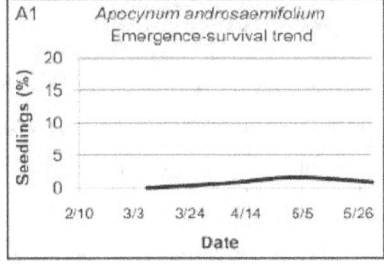

References

Drake et al. (1998), Gardenbed (2004), Gilky and Dennis (2001), Groen (2005), Hitchcock and Cronquist (1973), Johnson et al. (1998), Pojar and Mackinnon (1994), USDA FS (1988), USDA NRCS (2006).

Balsamorhiza careyana Gray
Carey's balsamroot
Asteraceae
BACA3

Balsamorhiza careyana is a long-lived, cool-season, perennial herb with a deep-seated, woody taproot. Basal leaves originating from a caudex are triangular, large, and green on both surfaces, sparsely hairy, cordate at base, 5–30 cm long and 5–10 cm wide. Multiple stems, each topped with one to multiple heads that radiate with a composite of disc and ray flowers having multiple overlapping bracts around base; fruit are achenes. Leaves of seedlings covered with fine hairs.

Distribution and habitat

Range is along the eastern Cascades from southern British Columbia to central Oregon. East of the Cascade Range, *B. careyana* can be found within the low and mid elevations from 300 to 1900 m, growing on open ridges, dry foothills, semiarid mountain rangelands, and on southerly exposures. Within its limited range, *B. careyana* occurs commonly in *Pinus ponderosa/Purshia tridentata/Festuca idahoensis* and dry *Pseudotsuga menziesii, Quercus,* and *Artemesia* associations in open sites that may become hot and dry. It grows on well-drained stony, silty, and loamy soils. Like *B. sagittata*, it is palatable to a wide range of wildlife. Prefers full sun but can grow in partial shade of canopy.

Reproductive ecology

Balsamorhiza species may take several years of growth to produce a flower in its natural habitat. *Balsamorhiza sagittata* is reported to exhibit self compatibility, but viable seed benefits from out-crossed pollen. Flowering occurs from late March through July. The flowers produce nectar that attracts insects and may be, like the nectar of *B. deltoidea,* high in sugar concentration. Flowers attract a variety of insects including bees, flies, and butterflies. Effective pollinators are small, solitary bees that rely on *B. careyana* for pollen. The fruit is a 3- to 4-sided hairless achene. Pollination may be sufficient for high rate of seed production, but the seeds may be heavily predated by insects; seed quality and viability are reduced by insect damage. Flowers can be subject to frost damage and seed heads are palatable to animals. The filled-seed rate of cleaned seeds collected at Green Ridge in 2004 was 49 percent and from seeds sampled directly from seed heads in 2005, was 9 percent (range 0–33 percent). The mean number of seeds per capitulum in 2005 was 57.2 (21–119). Seed dispersal may be primarily by animals. Seeds can be found on the ground near the parent plant; however, they may not persist in a seed bank. Like *B. sagittata*, *B. careyana* is long-lived and able to regenerate vegetatively after fire or other disturbance that does not destroy caudex or root crown.

Propagation

Before seeds were collected at the Green Ridge study site, the seedheads were checked to be sure fruit had matured and were dry. Dried seedheads were harvested by breaking off from stem and crushing them as they were placed into a paper bag. The seed heads were left to dry further in the bags in the lab for several days before cleaning. A crushing boat or No. 8 circular screen (3.2 mm) was used to break up flower heads followed by screening with a screen equivalent in hole size to about 5 mm (0.1953 in, 12.5/64) and air blown at 18 mm. Screens of various mesh size can be used to remove chaff. The screened seeds can be further separated in a South Dakota Seed Blower at an air velocity of about 3.5 m/s or other type of air screen or separator. Achenes may show evidence of insects or insect damage and should be checked for holes or frass. At a moisture content of 7.8 percent, the number of seeds collected at Green Ridge per kilogram was 93,130. Low moisture content increases seed longevity; cleaned dry seeds can be stored at 20 °C for up for 5 years; storing at near or below freezing may prolong viability. The stratification temperature should be at freezing or as close to freezing as possible. Optimum temperatures for germination are reported near those for stratification. Seed quality and viability can be reduced by insect damage. The viability of tetrazolium-tested study seeds was 79 percent; however, the rate of empty and damaged seed differed greatly among lots.

For large-scale sowing, seeds of *Balsamorhiza* species can be broadcast sown or drilled; however, because seeds are relatively large, they should be covered with soil. Sowing in fall or winter is preferable as *B. careyana* will germinate in cold soil and near-freezing temperatures. The mean germination of study seeds sown at Green Ridge based on accumulated emergence was 55.8 percent. Emergence was 7.0 percent in February, and by mid March, 44.8 percent. Percentage of surviving seedlings by late May

was 45.2 percent and the following May, 34.7 percent. Trend in first-year emergence and survival is shown in figure A2. By May of the second growing season, average length of the hairy basal leaves was 6.5 cm. Aerial growth is reported to be slow for this long-lived perennial plant, presumably, because much of the growth is being allocated to root growth, and may take anywhere from 3 to 8 years before the plant is mature enough to flower. Compared to the other 17 species at the Green Ridge site, *B. careyana* seeds had the highest germination; seedlings had among the best survival rates and afforded the greatest amount of cover. Seeds of this and other *Balsamorhiza* species are highly recommended for use in a seeding program.

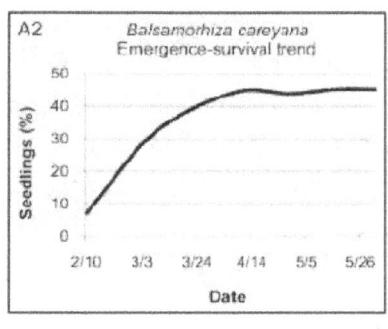

References

Cane (2005), Gilky and Dennis (2001), Hitchcock and Cronquist (1973), McWilliams (2002), Rose et al. (1998), USDA FS (1988), USDA NRCS (2006), USDI BLM (2003), Young and Evans (1979).

Various bees foraging on large, showy flower of *Calochortus macrocarpus* blooming on Green Ridge, eastside Cascades Range.

Calochortus macrocarpus Dougl.
Sagebrush mariposa lily
Liliaceae
CAMA5

Calochortus macrocarpus is a long-lived perennial monocot in the Lily family about 20–30 cm tall. It grows an erect stem from deep-seated, oval bulbs with slender, grass-like leaves and is one- to three-flowered. The flower has narrow green sepals and three broad, pale pink to lavender petals. The inner basal part of the petal has a dark purple band and is moderately bearded above the somewhat triangular nectar gland medially located toward the base of the petal, three stamens with anthers longer than the filaments; fruit linear and three-angled.

Distribution and habitat

Range extends across the Columbia River plateau from British Columbia south to northern California and east to Nevada and northwestern Montana and is found over much of the arid interior of the Pacific Northwest. *Calochortus macrocarpus* occurs in dry prairies or grasslands, sagebrush scrub or open *Pinus ponderosa* forest in well-drained, sandy or rocky soil at elevations as high as 2000 m. Palatable to livestock and ungulates. Distribution is increasingly patchy and probably has declined in abundance in grazed grasslands and prairies.

Reproductive ecology

Calochortus macrocarpus flowers in late May-June. The species may be able to self-pollinate and set fruit, but generally is pollinated by insect vectors. The large flowers attract a variety of insects to its pollen and nectar located in glands at the base of the corolla; however, they may be successfully pollinated only by large bees such as *Bombus* species. The fruit is a three-chambered capsule. Each chamber may have about a hundred flat, round disc-like seeds about ½ cm in diameter. Fruit set varies from year to year but can be > 60 percent. The mean filled-seed rate of the study seeds collected at Green Ridge in the east-side central Oregon Cascade Range was 90.0 percent in 2004 and 47.0 percent in 2005; mean number of seeds per capsule, 44.6 (range 3–122, N = 20). The species does not appear to be pollinator limited, but effective seed production fluctuates widely because the flowering and fruiting stems are browsed by deer and elk, in some years

so heavily that fruit is rare. Maturity from seedling to a flowering plant may take from 3 to 5 years. Some individuals in a population may become dormant in response to an environmental condition and not emerge every year. This should be taken into consideration when evaluating reintroductions of this species.

Propagation

Calochortus macrocarpus propagates readily from seed. When mature, seeds are disk-shaped, pale, straw-colored, and < 0.5 cm in diameter. Seeds are ready to collect in late August–early September from plants at Green Ridge on the east side of the central Oregon Cascade Range. After capsules are fully mature and beginning to dehisce by splitting starting at the apex, the papery seeds are easily collected and poured into paper bags. Seeds are relatively free of chaff but need to be blown at about 10 mm to remove empty seeds. Number of seeds per kilogram was 377,010. Seed viability by tetrazolium testing was 86 percent.

Stratification is required for ex situ germination; storage at below freezing temperatures is recommended. Study seeds from Green Ridge sown in late September had germinated before February with peak germination in mid March. Seedlings showed leaf damage from insect predation. Some seedlings recovered from the clipping and continued to produce leaves. Germination based on accumulated emergence was 54.7 percent, and survival by May 19 was 37 percent. The seasonal trend in emergence and survival is shown in figure A3. By the following May, survival was 24.7 percent. Emergence rate of seeds sown in a grass-sagebrush steppe in central Washington was 55 percent; however, for surface-sown seeds, emergence was 6 percent. When precipitation decreases and soil dries in late May, the aerial part of the plant senesces, which is characteristic of vernal monocots. Leaves averaged 6.5 cm and were longer in the second year than the first. However, for this large, liliaceous monocot, it may take from 3 to 5 years to produce a flowering plant from seed. Although some *Calochortus* species may be propagated from bulbs, the propagules of most do not successfully transplant from the wild. Collecting bulbs or flowering stems in the wild is discouraged or illegal because it destroys the entire plant.

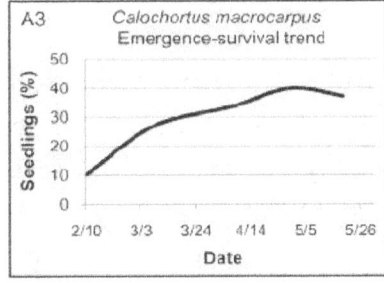

References

Durham and Sackschewsky (2004), Gardenbed (2004), Hitchcock and Cronquist (1973), Kruckeberg (1982), Miller et al. (2004), USDA NRCS (2006).

Erigeron filifolius (Hook.) Nutt. var. *filifolius*
Threadleaf fleabane
Asteraceae
ERFIF

Erigeron filifolius var. *filifolius* is a tall (10–50 cm), perennial herb with a taproot and many stiff, hairy branching stems and narrow, linear leaves (0.3–3.0 mm wide). Inflorescence may have single to multiple flower heads (1–4) with ray flowers (15–75) that are blue to pinkish white and 3–13 mm long; fruits are achenes with pappi and sparse hairs.

Distribution and habitat

The species ranges from British Columbia through eastern Oregon to the east side of the Cascades and south to northern California and east to Nevada and Wyoming. It occurs in sagebrush and dry forests, in plains and foothills at elevations 1200–2000 m. Adapted to dry, rocky, or sandy soil, and lava beds, it is associated with *Purshia tridentata, Artemesia* species, *Juniperus* species, and *Pinus ponderosa*.

Reproductive ecology

Erigeron filifolius flowers from June through August. Small generalist pollinators such as solitary bees and syrphid flies foraging for nectar and pollen visit the composite flowers. *Erigeron* species is also visited by wasps and butterflies attracted to the nectar. Some *Erigeron* species may be self-fertile; however, this species requires an insect vector for successful seed set, but may self-pollinate as well. Of the study plants from Green Ridge on the east-side central Oregon Cascade Range, the average number of achenes per seed head in 2005 was 134; mean rate of filled seed was 45.0 percent in 2004 and 11.6 percent in 2005. In both years, *E. filifolius* seeds showed evidence of predation.

Propagation

Seeds are collected at Green Ridge on the east side of the central Oregon Cascade Range from late July through mid August. Seeds remain in collection bags; each bag is inspected so as to avoid contamination of damaged or infested seeds. When the seeds are ready for collection from the seed heads, the pale and feathery pappi are highly visible, and along with the achenes are easily removed by hand without pulling off the seed head. Achenes are crushed using a crushing boat to de-hair seeds and screened with 0.0833-in (1/12) mesh screen. Seeds are air blown at 10 mm, then 13 mm, and screened again with 0.0833; repeat process if seeds still have pappi attached. The seeds are very tiny; number of seeds collected at Green Ridge per kilogram was 5.3 million at 7.2 percent moisture content. Mean seed viability of two seed lots was 85 percent, and mean rate of in vitro seed germination (no stratification) 35.3 percent. Stratification at almost freezing temperatures might increase germination rate. Mean germination of seeds sown in September at Green Ridge based on accumulated emergence was 11.0 percent; survival by late May was 1.4 percent. For trend in emergence and survival see figure A4. Frost heaving of soil in early months may have contributed to poor emergence rate. Two-year survival was 1.2 percent with little or no aerial growth; height was < 1 cm. This species germinated very early in spring at near-freezing temperatures, but the small seeds are vulnerable to frost heaving. Grows best in full sun; drought tolerant.

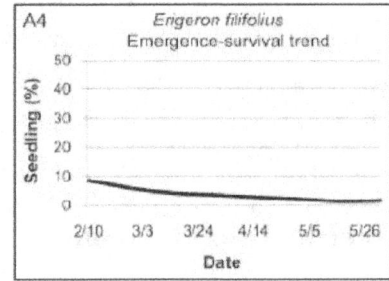

References

Gilky and Dennis (2001), Harmond et al. (1968), Hitchcock and Cronquist (1973), Parkinson (2003), USDA NRCS (2006), USDI BLM (2003).

Eriogonum umbellatum Torr.
Sulphur-flower buckwheat
Polygonaceae
ERUM

Eriogonum umbellatum is a low-growing branching perennial herb or semi-shrub from a strong taproot with branching crown. Stems prostrate, branching and mat forming or erect; leaves variable oblong to oval or spatulate. The species is highly variable in its vegetative and floral characters. The inflorescence is simple to compound umbel of dominantly light-yellow flowers borne on a short axis surrounded by a greenish campanulate involucre on slender pedicels. Perianth cream or yellow, becoming accented with shades of orange or pink. Flowers are often imperfect. Three styles bear a one-celled ovary and single ovule. Fruit is a smooth, three-angled, achene.

Distribution and habitat

Range from southern British Columbia south to California east of the Cascade Range, east to Montana and Wyoming, and south to Arizona. Mostly occurs in sagebrush steppe, dry prairie or alpine rocky ridges, mountain slopes from sea level to subalpine elevations. Occurs in dry open areas under full sunlight, with minimal rainfall and rocky to sandy, moderately coarse, well-drained soil. Associated with *Artemesia*, *Purshia*, and bunchgrasses in dry *Pinus ponderosa* associations.

Reproductive ecology

Flowering from May through August, depending upon topography and variation in climate. Maximum seed set is dependent on insect pollination, although autogamy may occur. Pollen and nectar attract wasps, bees, and other insects. For each flower, a hard, dry, single-seeded achene is produced. Achenes mature in 6–8 weeks. Birds and small mammals (quail, deer, grouse) consume the seeds. May be host to caterpillars of a copper butterfly (*Lycaena gorgon*) known to lay eggs on flower stems of *Eriogonum* species. A single umbel may have many seeds, but the rate of filled seeds may be low and vary greatly among lots and years. In 2004, the mean filled-seed rate of study seeds originating from Green Ridge on the east-side central Oregon Cascade Range was 71.7 percent and in 2005, 17.3 percent.

Propagation

The dry, papery umbels are collected at Green Ridge from late July through August and placed into paper bags. Mature seeds (pappus visible) are easily removed by hand without pulling off the seed head. Seed heads are crushed with a crushing boat or by hand, screened with 4 by 30 mesh (0.0203-in) screen, and air blown at 30 mm. Screen with No. 10 Westrup screen or repeat with 0.188 or 1/16 hand screen or 0.1094-in round screen and 0.0203-in screen to aid stem removal (Harmand et al. 1968). Because the percentage of filled seed may be low, cleaning requires repeated screening and blowing to rid seed of flower chaff and separate the empty from filled seed. The number of study seeds collected at Green Ridge per kilogram was 291,000 at 8.8 percent moisture content. Germination rate of 86 percent was reported on unstratified seeds from Ada County, Idaho, and seedling survival under greenhouse conditions was 52 percent. The mean viability of the study seeds from Green Ridge based on tetrazolium testing was 72.5 percent; germination rate of unstratified seeds on moist filter paper was 37.2 percent with 42.4 visibly moldy. Stratification requirements vary greatly depending upon origin of seed. Usually the higher the elevation the more stratification required. At the Green Ridge study site, seeds began germinating early under cold soil conditions. Emergence in early February 2005 was 9.6 percent. Germination based on accumulated emergence was 34.5 percent with germination peaking roughly in mid March. See figure A5 for trend over one growing season in emergence and survival. Seedlings are morphologically adapted to cold and high solar irradiance but are susceptible to damping-off fungi and insect herbivory (see photo). Mean survival was 21.6 percent in May at the end of the first growing season and the following year, 11.3 percent. Average height was 2.3 cm by May of the second year, and contribution to herbaceous cover was low. Approximately 0.2 lb of seeds collected at Green Ridge and sown in fall for growout at Lucky Peak Nursery, Boise, Idaho, yielded 25.0 lb in 2 years and about 5.5 lb of seed the year following (appendix 1).

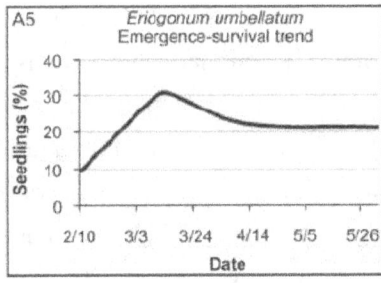

A5 — *Eriogonum umbellatum* Emergence-survival trend

References

Archibald (2006), Gilky and Dennis (2001), Harmond et al. (1968), Hitchcock and Cronquist (1973), Parkinson (2003), Parkinson and DeBolt (2005a), Rose et al. (1998), USDA NRCS (2006).

Eriophyllum lanatum (Pursh) Forbes
Common woolly sunflower
Asteraceae
ERLA6

Eriophyllum lanatum is a perennial herb or subshrub 10–40 cm tall, several stemmed, with woolly leaves alternate and variable from entire to ternate. Heads radiate with few ray flowers, involucre with two series of bracts, disk flowers few to many, perfect; ray flowers 8–13, yellow (1–2 cm). Achene, slender, four angled. Variable species morphology with numerous varieties.

Distribution and habitat

Eriophyllum lanatum ranges from British Columbia to California and east to Montana and Utah. It occurs in low to mid elevation in prairies and mountainous dry forests. *Eriophyllum lanatum* grows well in dry, open slopes or rocky outcrops and occurs on hillsides or lowlands in well-drained soil.

Reproductive ecology

Eriophyllum lanatum is an outcrossing species that exhibits considerable polyploidy. Polyploidy can give rise to ecotypes that may be specifically adapted to environmental conditions. *Eriophyllum lanatum* flowers from April through May. The foliage and buds appear to exude a substance before flowers open that is highly attractive to flies. Flies visit the plant before the flower opens and appear to be feeding on a sticky exudate from the calyx. The flowers are visited by a variety of insects for pollen and nectar but flies were the most constant visitors. The mean number of seeds collected from the capitula was 75 (N = 8, range 57–86); mean rate of filled seed in 2004 was 71.0 percent and in 2005, 57.8 percent.

Propagation

At the Green Ridge site on the east-side Oregon Cascade Range, seeds are collected when the seed heads are dry and petals shriveled in late August. One way to collect seeds is to remove seed heads with scissors below the calyx, which is less destructive than removing by hand. Seed heads placed in paper bags can remain in bags in the lab for further drying. If seed heads are sufficiently dry, the seeds readily fall out of the receptacle when touched or shaken into paper bags. Insect predation of the achenes does occur with this species. However, we found less insect predation of *E. lanatum* achenes at the Green Ridge site than at a site in the central Willamette Valley-Coast Range foothills. Seeds were cleaned in the Westrup machine with No. 10 or 12 screen followed by air blowing at 20 mm. Seeds cleaned the following year were also screened sequentially with 3/64 by 5/16, 18/20, 20/20 for seed, and 36/36 for dust, and air blown at 16-18 or 22 mm. The number of cleaned seeds per kilogram was 1,387,900 at 5.6 percent moisture content. Mean viability of two cleaned seed lots by tetrazolium testing was 59 percent.

Seeds sown at Green Ridge in late September 2004 emerged in early March 2005 when diurnal soil temperatures began to rise to above freezing. The germination rate based on accumulated emergence of seedlings was 16.9 percent. By the end of May, seedling survival was 13.9 percent and was 5.9 percent by May of the following year. The trend in emergence and survival in first growing season is shown in figure A6. Average height was 3.1 cm; however most growth is through lateral branching. Cover was maintained from 2005 to 2006 owing to vegetative spread of surviving seedlings. This species grows and matures rapidly and provides excellent cover because of its spreading habit as shown in photo of an *E. lanatum* subplot at the Green Ridge study site. This species is productive also in a nursery setting. At the Lucky Peak Nursery, Boise, Idaho, 0.1 lb of seed yielded 32.0 lb of seed in the second growing year.

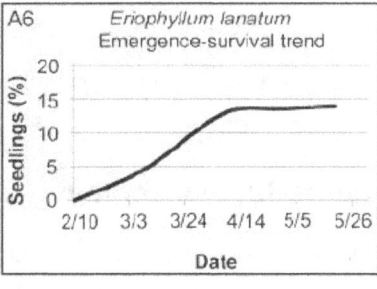

References

Archibald (2006), Gilky and Dennis (2001), Harmond et al. (1968), Hitchcock and Cronquist (1973), Parkinson (2003), Rose et al. (1998), USDA NRCS (2006), USDI BLM (2003), Vance et al. (2006).

Linum lewisii Pursh
Lewis flax
Linaceae
LILE2

Linum lewisii is a short-lived perennial herb or subshrub having a semi-woody rootstock producing one or several stems 10–70 cm in height. The inflorescences are cymose with five-petaled flowers pale to nearly white to sky blue. The homostylous flower has five petals and five fused carpels, each with two ovules.

Distribution and habitat

Linum lewisii ranges throughout western North America from Alaska to New Mexico. It occurs in a range of habitats from prairies and shrub steppe to dry forests and alpine ridges on open or partly shaded sites with generally dry, well-drained soil.

Reproductive ecology

Linum lewisii is an obligate outcrosser. Flowers are produced throughout summer and early autumn, and each flower opens in the morning and blooms for a single day. The species attracts bees and flies, which are attracted to both nectar and pollen. The most common visitors at high elevation in Colorado are small solitary bees and muscoid flies although syrphid flies and rarely *Bombus* species were reported carrying *Linum* pollen. At the Green Ridge site on the east-side central Oregon Cascade Range, small flies and solitary bees were observed visiting the flowers. The fruit are round capsules each containing two seeds. Reproductive success was high. In 2 years of sampling and cutting seed, we never found one that was not filled. *Linum lewisii* seeds have a complex and conditional dormancy (see Meyer and Kitchen 1994). Meyer and Kitchen reported that variable germination responses in the field for seeds from the same origins, whether in the fall, spring, or the following year may depend on environmental conditions interacting with the seeds' dormancy response allowing this native flax species to be highly adaptable to the variable conditions of the montane and high plateau regions of the Western United States.

Propagation

Racemes of *L. lewisii* are grasped below the seed heads and tipped into paper bags or buckets. Mature seeds readily fall from the capsules into the container and clean easily. For complete cleaning, crush capsules to release seeds, hand screen with 0.087-in (1/12–1/14) screens and air blow. The number of seeds per kilogram was 334,610 at a 6.9 percent moisture content. The mean filled-seed rate was 100 percent. Seed dormancy is highly variable and will differ among sources. *Linum lewisii* can be seeded in early spring but recommend seeding in late fall. Seeds sown in late September at Green Ridge on the east side of the central Oregon Cascade Range germinated in early March when soil temperatures were near freezing and while soil retained moisture. The mean germination based on accumulated emergence was 34.3 percent; peak emergence was in early April, and by late May, survival rate of seedlings was 29.4 percent as shown by trend line in figure A7. In May the following year, survival was 25.6 percent. However, new seedlings emerged in over half the plots (1–8 per plot). Average height in 2006 was 8.2 cm (1.4–24.6 cm). Large variation is because of bolting of maturing plants and new recruitment in 2006. Individuals that reached maturity and flowered in 2006 averaged about 25 cm in height. Average vegetative cover was 4.4 percent in 2005 and rose to 12.7 percent in 2006 because 20 percent of the plants had bolted and flowered. In a nursery environment with ample water and fertilizer, fall-seeded *L. lewisii* can produce flowers within a single growing season. The yield of seeds from 0.1 lb of seed sown at Lucky Peak Nursery, Boise, Idaho, was relatively low; plants produced only about 0.55 lb of seed in the second year and none the third year. Seeds of this species have been shown to have variable dormancy and widely variable germination rates. More studies are needed on this species, as it is excellent for a seeding program because of its rapid growth, maturity, and low mortality.

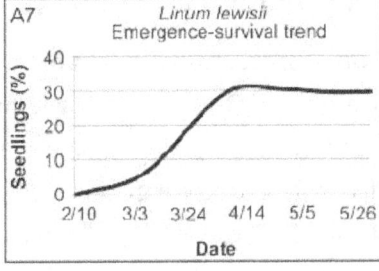

References

Hitchcock and Cronquist (1973), Kearns and Inouye (1994), Meyer and Kitchen (1994), Pendleton et al. (2008), Reeves (2006), USDA FS (1988), USDA NRCS (2006).

Lomatium triternatum (Pursh) Coult. & Rose
Nineleaf biscuit root
Apiaceae
LOTR2

Lomatium triternatum is a perennial forb/herb; stems usually solitary 20–80 cm tall, from a simple or sometimes branched crown on an elongated taproot. Leaves are mostly basal and cleft several times, each leaf cleft into three long, narrow leaflets, up to 10 cm long. Inflorescence is a bractless, compound umbel with small clusters of yellow flowers, bracts green. Fruits are schizocarps, oblong to elliptic, flattened, with papery side wings, two flat, ribbed seeds.

Distribution and habitat

Range is from British Columbia and Alberta to Colorado, Utah, and California. One of the most common and widespread plants found in a scattered distribution in plains and foothills on open slopes in *P. ponderosa* forest types. Scattered and locally common at low to mid elevations but can be found at elevations as high as 3000 m (10,000 ft) in Wyoming. *Lomatium triternatum* prefers well-drained soil and full sun to partial shade.

Reproductive ecology

The hermaphroditic flowers depend on pollinators for seed set, and are a source of pollen and possibly also nectar to insects, particularly solitary bees, wasps (such as the cuckoo wasp shown on the umbel) and syrphid flies. The mean number of Green Ridge seeds per umbel was 69 (range 31–262, N = 20); mean rate of filled seeds was 73.3 percent in 2004 and 86.5 percent in 2005 indicating pollination is effective. However, fruits and seeds may be predated by weevils which are patchily distributed within a large population of *L. triternatum*.

Propagation

Fruit and seeds of *L. triternatum* are ready for collecting when they no longer feel waxy to the touch. *Lomatium triternatum* is typically scattered and not abundant in any one area. Seeds are removed by running fingers upward along the stem and pulling gently. Seeds are placed in paper bags and brought inside for further drying. Seeds were cleaned by hand screening and blowing off any chaff. The number of cleaned seeds per kilogram of seeds collected from Green Ridge in Jefferson County, Oregon, was 145,160 at a moisture content of 7.9 percent. Viability of cleaned seeds using tetrazolium testing was 77 percent. In vitro germination of stratified seeds was only 16 percent with a low percentage of moldy seeds; many seeds germinated while in stratification. Seeds from Malheur County, Oregon, also were germinated in the dark under stratification at 4 °C; under greenhouse conditions, survival was 53 percent. Germination based on accumulative emergence of seeds collected and grown at the Green Ridge study site on the east-side Oregon Cascade Range, was 70.8 percent with seedling survival by May, 45.1 percent. The trend in emergence and survival is shown in figure A8. Survival 1 year later was 35.8 percent, and average height of surviving seedlings was 10.1 cm (6.2–14.2 cm). The tallest plants bore flowering stems. This is a cold-season species in which germination of the Green Ridge study seeds was already > 35 percent by early February (when soil temperatures were usually at or below freezing) reaching its peak by mid March. Others have reported that stored seed can be rather slow to germinate; however, this was one of the 3 out of 18 study species at Green Ridge that in some instances matured to flowering in the first year.

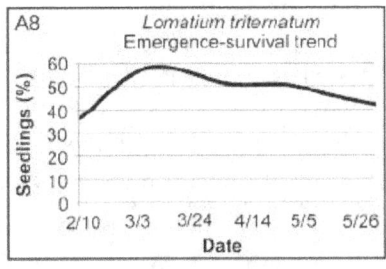

A8 *Lomatium triternatum* Emergence-survival trend

References

Gardenbed (2004), Hitchcock and Cronquist (1973), Parkinson and DeBolt (2005b), Thompson and Pellmyr (1989), USDA FS (1988), USDA NRCS (2006).

Lotus crassifolius (Benth.) Greene
Big deervetch
Fabaceae
LOCR

Lotus crassifolius is a rhizomatous, perennial herb or subshrub. Growth form from semi-prostrate to upright, up to 1 m tall, erect to spreading, and branching. Leaves are pinnately compound with 5–15 oblong leaflets. Inflorescence an umbel with 7–20 flowers on short pedicels, flowers white or greenish-yellow tinged with reddish purple; fruit dehiscent, elongated legume, 2–5 cm long, with 4–20 dark brown, round seeds.

Distribution and habitat

Ranges from northwest Washington to southern California and in the Cascade Range from low to middle elevations. Occurs in scattered stands. Common habitat may be dry to mesic in *P. ponderosa* associations and mixed coniferous forests along streambanks or in open areas with deep Well-drained soil.

Reproductive ecology

Flowers bloom May-July. Nectar and pollen attract bees. Legumes mature from mid-July through August at Green Ridge on the east-side central Oregon Cascade Range. Pods twist spirally at maturity and halves split with force expelling seed. The seeds are hard, round, and about 20–30 mm in diameter. The mean number of Green Ridge seeds per legume was 10.8 (range 4–20, N = 20) and mean rate of filled seeds was 60.3 percent. Fruits and seed coats were visibly damaged by insects; however, examination of cut seeds indicated that predation did appear to affect the endosperm or embryo. Lotus seeds reported to have been partially eaten by a weevil seed predator were tested for viability, and subsequent seedling vigour and a large proportion of the damaged seeds were found to be viable. Like other species in the Fabaceae family, seeds require scarification as well as stratification for best germination. Perhaps the weevil acts as a scarifier. *Lotus crassifolius* also reproduces vegetatively from rhizomes following wildfire or other disturbances.

Propagation

Seeds are collected when fruit appears reddish tan and dry to the touch. The mature legumes are removed from the plant or broken into paper bags held below the plants. Seeds are easy to clean and can be readily cleaned by hand or with the help of Westrup machine and No. 5 screen. An air blower at 5 mm can be used to separate chaff, if necessary. The number of clean seeds per kilogram of seeds collected at Green Ridge was 88,230 at a moisture content of 7.9 percent. The mean viability of seeds of all three lots was about 95 percent.

Lotus crassifolius seeds benefit from stratification and should be fall planted so they can stratify in situ. We investigated whether scarification and using a soaking time longer than 24 h would also help in vitro germination. Scarification (light sanding of seed coat) and 10-week stratification with a 24- or 48-h soak significantly improved seed germination (42.6 percent vs. < 30.0 percent). Scarification and soaking does not help germination if seeds are not stratified, as germination of unstratified seeds was < 0.5 percent even with those additional treatments.

Lotus crassifolius seeds sown in late September at the Green Ridge study site began germinating in mid March when minimum soil temperatures and average air temperatures were above freezing. Germination based on accumulated emergence was 22.4 percent. Emergence increased from March through May as shown by the trend curve in figure A9. Survival in late May was 21.7 percent. Survival in May the following year was 1.1 percent. The drastic drop in survival appeared to be primarily caused by insect herbivory as shown in photo of *L. crassifolius* seedling in plot. Because of the drastic drop in number of viable seedlings, average height of this normally fast-growing, herb was only 2.0 cm in the second year, and cover declined to 0.4 percent indicating that *L. crassifolius* seedlings were seriously affected by insect predators. *Lotus crassifolius* seeds from Green Ridge, Deschutes National Forest sown at the Lucky Peak nursery grew rapidly and increased seed yield from 0.4 lb to 15.5 lb in 3 years, an increase of > 3,700 percent. This species has excellent potential to produce cover and occupy a site under conditions where herbivory does not severely impact seedlings.

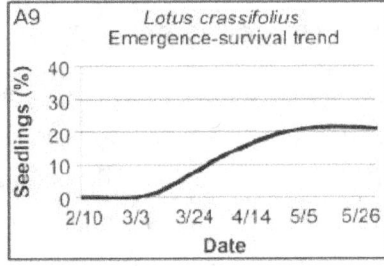

References

Flessner and Darris (2001), Hitchcock and Cronquist (1973), Ollerton and Lack (1996), USDA FS (1988), USDA NRCS (2006).

Olsynium douglasii (A. Dietr.) Bickn.
Douglas' grass widow
Iridaceae
OLDOD

Olsynium douglasii is a rhizomatous, perennial monocot with stems 10–30 cm tall; often found in clumps with narrow but flattened grass-like leaves rarely more than 10 cm long, sheathed at the base. Perianth of flower is a deep reddish purple with 6 tepals up to 3 cm long, three stamens fused at base with bright yellow anthers. The ovary is inferior; fruit are three-celled somewhat globose capsules up to 1 cm long with several seeds per cell. Seeds are about 1.5–2.5 mm, brown, angular and pitted. *Olsynium douglasii* var. *inflatum* is often lighter in color with wider perianth and more inflated filament tube at base than var. *douglasii*.

Distribution and habitat

Olsynium douglasii ranges from British Columbia south along both sides of the Cascade Range to California and along the Columbia River gorge, east to Idaho and Utah. Occurs from near sea level to about 1800 m, in prairies and dry western forest types including pine and oak woodlands, also in dry sagebrush and juniper steppe. A cool-season plant that prefers open areas where there is sufficient moisture in the spring.

Reproductive ecology

Olsynium douglasii is the only member of the genus found in North America and the only one that offers nectar in addition to pollen. It flowers from February through June depending upon elevation. The flowers tend to be ephemeral opening for a few hours. *Bombus* and *Osmia* species as well as other species of solitary bees visit the flower for nectar and pollen. Because pollinating insects rely on nectar for energy in early spring, *O. douglasii* may be an important energy source. The mean filled-seed rate of seeds collected from Green Ridge on the east-side central Oregon Cascade Range was 89.0 percent indicating pollination was effective.

Propagation

Seeds are collected by tipping the dried and dehiscent capsules into paper bags without removing the capsules or the plant from the ground. Seeds empty into the bag easily without much chaff. Hand screening may be all that is needed to clean seed. The number of dry, cleaned seeds per kilogram was about 293,460; moisture content was not determined. Seed viability of the single Green Ridge seed lot was 79 percent. The germination rate of the study seeds on Green Ridge based on accumulated emergence was about 45 percent. The germination rate was higher than that reported by Kruckeberg (1982) who described seed germination as "dependably low" (10 to 20 percent). Seeds began to germinate in the field in early March. Germination was rapid, peaking by mid April. See figure A10 for trend in emergence and survival. Germination based on accumulated emergence was 45.0 percent and mean survival by late May was 29.8 percent. Mean survival in May the following year was 22.3 percent and average leaf length was 6.2 cm. Each seedling consisted of one, or possibly two, slender, grass-like leaves. The leaves had senesced by June when precipitation is low and the temperature elevates. No plants reached maturity. This species would not be used to increase vegetative cover but for its attractiveness to early spring pollinators and functional ability to grow with graminoids and broad-leaved plants. Vegetative propagation using offshoots from rhizomes has not been tested on a large scale but may be an option for increasing seed plants as they reportedly transplant well.

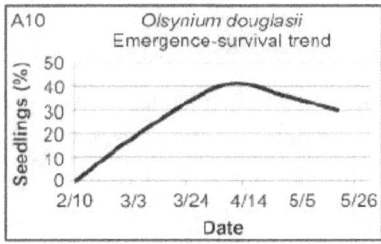

A10 — *Olsynium douglasii* Emergence-survival trend

References

Gilky and Dennis (2001), Goldblatt and Manning (2009), Hitchcock and Cronquist (1973), Kruckeberg (1982), Legler (2006), USDA NRCS (2006).

Penstemon humilis Nutt. ex Gray
Low beardtongue
Scrophulariaceae
PEHU

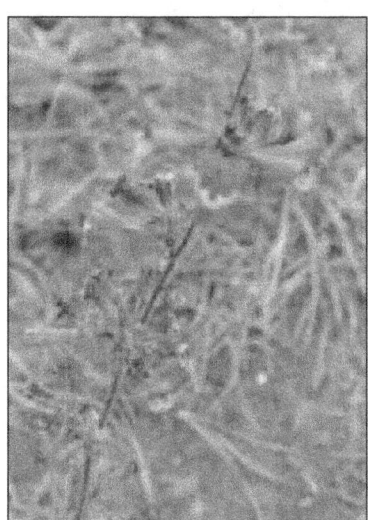

Penstemon humilis is a perennial herb about 10–60 cm tall with entire, lanceolate leaves up to 12 cm long and basal leaves tufted and persistent; inflorescence one or a few flowers, five-segmented calyx, the tips slightly purple, the corolla hairy, blue-purple. Pollen sacs glabrous opposite and dark and bearded staminode; inferior ovary; capsule length, 4–6 mm; seeds, 1–1.5 mm long.

Distribution and habitat

Range west of the Continental Divide from Washington to California, east to western Wyoming and Colorado. Species occurs on open, rocky and depauperate slopes in sagebrush prairies and valleys and dry open forests. Often found on road cuts along unpaved roads in *Pinus ponderosa/Purshia tridentata/Festuca idahoensis* associations.

Reproductive ecology

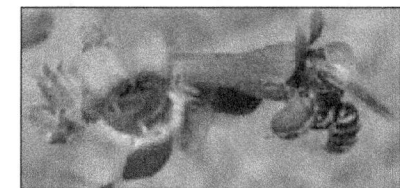

The small flower with its deep blue corolla and nectar glands attract moths and long-tongued bees such as the native leaf cutter bee (Megachilidae) shown in photo. Each capsule contains two dozen or more seeds. Little predation was observed of 60 sampled and cut seeds collected from Green Ridge for study; mean filled-seed rate was 83.3 percent. Flowering occurs from May through July; seeds mature about 6–8 weeks later. Seed distribution may be by animals or water, although rodents and birds eat seeds.

Propagation

Seeds are collected by carefully tipping the dried racemes with ripe fruit into paper bags without removing the dry capsules from the stem or pulling the plant from the ground. Seeds empty into the bag easily without much chaff. The small, hard seeds are easily cleaned by screening and may be air blown at 10 mm if needed. The number of seeds per kilogram of study seeds from Green Ridge on the east-side central Oregon Cascade Range was 4,822,100. Seed viability based on tetrazolium testing was 88 percent; mean in vitro germination rate of unstratified seeds was 37.2 percent with 42.4 percent of seeds eventually becoming moldy. Dry seeds in cold storage are reported to retain their viability well. Germination based on accumulated emergence of study seeds sown in late September at Green Ridge was 18.3 percent. Peak emergence occurred in late April. See figure A11 for trend in emergence and survival over the first growing season. Attrition resulted in 10.6 percent survival by late May, and by May the following year, 0.8 percent. Low survival appeared to be due in part to frost heaving that buried tiny seeds or displaced them to the soil surface where high soil surface temperatures may have also contributed to mortality. Cover was < 1 percent and height was observed to be ≤ 1 cm. This species may require more seeds under nursery rearing conditions. Other *Penstemon* species have reportedly been successfully propagated, but differences in dormancy among seed sources can be critical in this species.

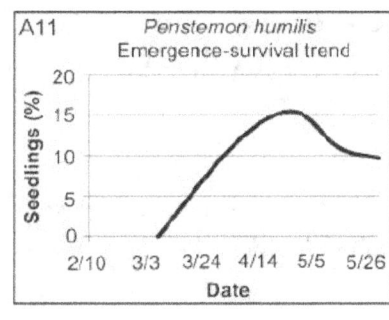

References

Clinebell and Bernhardt (1998), Gilky and Dennis (2001), Hitchcock and Cronquist (1973), Lodewick and Lodewick (1999), Meyer et al. (1995).

Silene douglasii Hook. var. *douglasii*
Douglas' silene
Caryophyllaceae
SIDOD

Silene douglasii var. *douglasii* is a caespitose, perennial herb 10–40 cm tall with linear-lanceolate leaves grouped at the base, a stout taproot and branching caudex. Stems are simple or few-branched with several pairs of sessile leaves at intervals up the stem. The inflorescence is cymose with axillary and terminal, white to pink flowers, calyx five-lobed, 10-nerved and tubular; petals five, bi-lobed and curl inward toward the end of 4–5 days of flowering; flower has 10 stamens and 3–4 styles. The fruit is a single-celled capsule, seeds 1–2 mm long, ovoid to round and brown, having rugose or bumpy surface with rounded papillate margins.

Distribution and habitat

Range from British Columbia south through Cascades to Sierra Nevada in central California, east to northern Utah, Nevada, and western Montana. Occurs in moist microsites in sagebrush steppe and prairie, and dry, montane forests on slopes and valleys under partial canopy.

Reproductive ecology

Silene douglasii is a source of pollen and nectar attracting the noctuid moth *Hadena variolata*, but also syrphid flies and halictid bees. Seedling recruitment is low as indicated by the low abundance and infrequent clusters of *S. douglasii* distributed throughout the collection area. Seed germination was significantly better in seeds produced from cross pollination than from self pollination. Pollinators are important to fecundity, but pollinating moths of genus *Hadena* also oviposit in flowers and their larvae predate capsules.

Interestingly, the seeds from capsules with the highest number of seeds collected from Green Ridge on the east-side central Oregon Cascade Range were more likely to be empty. Some seeds had holes in them and probably had been predated by larvae. Predation by noctuid moths is common in other *Silene* species and may stimulate new flowering. The mean number of seeds per capsule was 51.7 (range 20–95, N = 20). The filled-seed rate of seeds collected from capsules in 2005 was 78.0 percent.

Propagation

Dried seeds of the plant were collected at Green Ridge by tipping over the fruited stalks into paper bags without removing the capsules or the plant from the ground. Mature seeds from dehiscent capsules emptied into the bag easily without much chaff. In the lab, capsules were crushed releasing seeds onto a hand screen followed by air blowing. The small seeds numbered about 1.5 million seeds/kg or 692,591/lb; seed moistue content was 9.3 percent. Seed viability was high (90 percent) based on standard tetrazolium tests. Seeds will germinate in cool temperatures with germination occurring by early March when mean soil temperature was about 5 °C. Germination based on accumulated emergence of seeds sown the previous September was 23.1 percent. Survival was 12.7 percent and 1 year later was 4.1 percent. See the trend in emergence and survival in the first growing year shown in figure A12. Cover was less than 2 percent both years and measurable height the second year averaged 2.7 cm. This species grew slowly under the conditions of the site but it may be a slow-growing species. Domestic species are known to grow readily from seed. Seeds from the wild *S. douglasii* also can be greatly increased in a nursery setting. Seeds collected at Green Ridge were sown at the Lucky Peak Nursery, Boise, Idaho, resulting in 0.08 lb of seed yielding 13.5 lbs of seed the second year after sowing and 0.5 lb the third year for a total increase of >17,000 percent. Mature plants of other *Silene* species also have been propagated through division and cuttings. *Silene douglasii* needs to be monitored beyond 2 years, as it provides excellent cover at maturity and appears to be a relatively long-lived species that maintains itself through sprouting new shoots from a branching caudex.

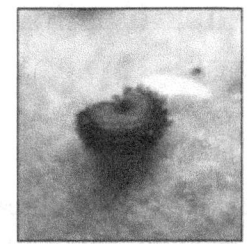

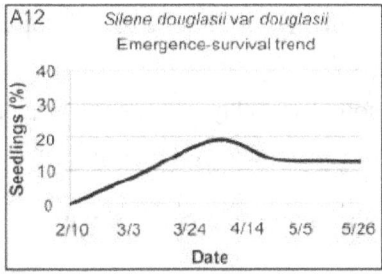

A12 *Silene douglasii var douglasii* Emergence-survival trend

References

Burgett et al. (1989), Hitchcock and Cronquist (1973), Kephart et al. (2006), Kruckeberg (1982), Lofflin and Kephart (2005), Pettersson (1991), USDA NRCS (2006), Wright and Meagher (2003).

Zigadenus venenosus S. Wats.
Meadow death camas
Liliaceae
ZIVE

Zigadenus venenosus is a cool-season, perennial monocot; grows from an oval bulb, stem 20–70 cm tall. Leaves mostly basal, grasslike, 10–30 cm long. Inflorescence an upright raceme with creamy-white tepals, campanulate flowers. Hypogynous with capsule 8–15 mm long, seeds light brown, 5–6 mm long.

Distribution and habitat

Ranges from British Columbia south to Baja California east to Alberta and south to Colorado. Grows in open forests and forest edges, meadows and rocky or grassy slopes usually at 400 to 3500 m elevations in a variety of soils from clay textured to gravelly or rocky. This species is often common in the ponderosa pine-bunchgrass plant communities.

Reproductive ecology

Zigadenus venenosus may require 2–3 years to attain sexual maturity. Flower parts persist until the capsule dehisces and seeds are dispersed. The flower requires an insect vector to produce viable seed. Despite that, *Z. venenosus* contains zygacine, putatively toxic to mammals and most bees. Adults of the generalist solitary bee, *Osmia lignaria* (Megachilidae), were paralyzed and soon after died when experimentally fed zygacine, which may explain the lack of native bee generalist pollinators visiting *Zigadenus* species. *Zigadenus* is pollinated by the solitary bee *Andrena astragali,* known as the death camas bee because it uses only *Zigadenus* pollen to feed itself and its progeny. Capsules and seeds are predated as shown in photo. The filled-seed rate was 82.2 percent of seeds sampled from the collection bags; some seeds were empty but none showed damage.

Propagation

Seeds mature from mid July through late August. To collect seeds, the dried, dehiscing racemes are snipped or carefully broken off by hand and placed into paper bags without removing the capsules. Seeds empty into the bag easily without much chaff. A crushing boat is used to break up flower heads and release seeds. Seeds are screened with 0.1641 (101/2) screens, then air separated with a blower at 18–25 mm max. Cleaned seeds per kilogram of study seeds from east-side central Oregon Cascades Range was 285,770. Five seed lots from different zones within the collection area were tested for viability; mean viability was 86 percent (74–92 percent). Seeds germinated during the 10 weeks in stratification confounding the in vitro germination test; no unstratified seeds germinated. Some of the seeds sown at Green Ridge in the fall had germinated before mid February indicating tolerance of cold soil and air temperatures. Germination of study seeds sown at Green Ridge based on accumulated seedling emergence was 44.2 percent; survival of emergent seedlings by late May was 32.7 percent. See figure A13 for trend in emergence and survival in the first growing year. By May the following year, survival was 25.6 percent and average leaf length of surviving seedlings was 5.8 cm. *Zigadenus* may be propagated vegetatively also by carefully extracting bulb offsets from its bulb located about 5–20 cm underground.

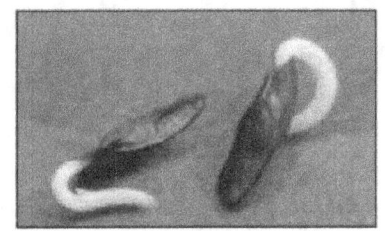

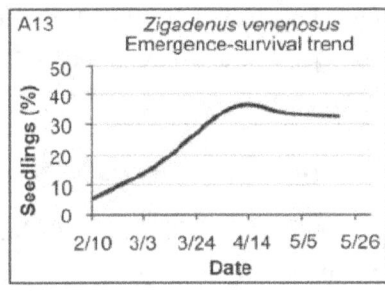

A13 *Zigadenus venenosus*
Emergence-survival trend

References

Cane et al. (2004), Gilky and Dennis (2001), Hitchcock and Cronquist (1973), Howard (1992), Tepedino (2003), USDA NRCS (2006).

Achnatherum thurberianum (Piper) Barkworth
Thurber's needle grass
Poaceae
ACTH7

Achnatherum thurberianum is a strongly tufted perennial, bunchgrass with culms, 30–60 cm tall, sheath glabrous, ligules 3–6 mm, blades 10–25 cm long, filiform and involute. Inflorescence is a long, narrow panicle having few flowers. Glumes are 9–14 mm long, floret 7–9 mm, lemma 8–9 mm and awn 4–5 cm long, jointed with hairs 1–2 mm long on lower joints. Fruit are caryopses.

Distribution and habitat

Range from Washington and Oregon east to central Idaho and southwestern Montana, south to Nevada and central California; occurs on grassland prairies, open coniferous forest, sagebrush steppe on rocky slopes. Associated with *Pinus ponderosa*, *Juniperus* spp. and *Festuca idahoensis* and *Pseudoroegnaria spicata* where it is a common subordinate of those grass communities. The species is better adapted to, and can be the dominant grass in, warmer and drier sites. One of the most drought-tolerant species, *A. thurberianum* grows in warm soil and in sagebrush habitat, and is typically the dominant grass in the driest sites. However *A. thurberianum* generally recovers slowly following wildfire and may have reduced vigor. Competitive perennial and annual grasses, especially the invasive exotic, *Bromus tectorum*, which is a highly successful competitor of *A. thurberianum,* seedlings can inhibit its postburn reestablishment.

Reproductive ecology

Achnatherum thurberianum flowers from May through June and is wind pollinated. Seeds disperse to provide new recruits, and tillering vegetatively expands the existing plant; however, if root crown is burned, *A. thurberianum* will only reproduce by seed. *A. thurberianum* is not as adapted to cold soil, and to germinate, it requires higher soil and air temperatures than either *Festuca idahoensis* or *Pseudoroegnaria spicata*. The filled-seed rate of seed collected from Green Ridge was 60.0 percent in 2004 and 61.6 percent in 2005. However seed production has been reported as generally low.

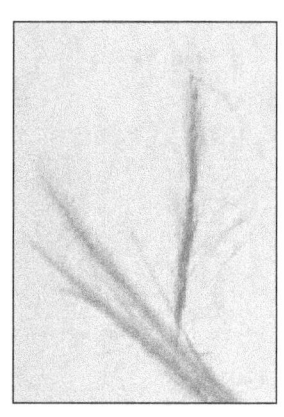

Propagation

Seeds are collected by hand July–August, placed in paper bags, and allowed to continue to dry inside in a dry room. Seeds are de-awned and cleaned using a Westrup machine with No. 14 screen, three times using a hard brush and a 3 by 5/16 screen on the clipper with ½ airflow. The number of Green Ridge seeds per kilogram was 485,950 at 9.9 percent moisture content. Seed viability by tetrazolium testing was 92 percent. Literature reports a maximum germination rate of 25 percent and optimum germination temperature of 15–25 °C (59–77 °F). The mean germination by in vitro germination testing of the study seeds using standard conditions was 64.8 percent. Seeds placed in a furrow and covered germinated and survived better than those broadcast seeded. Seeds sown in late September at Green Ridge did not begin to germinate until soil temperatures had warmed to 10 °C (50 °F). Germination based on accumulated emergence was 32.8 percent; survival was 29.0 percent, and the following year, 13.4 percent. Trend in emergence and survival over the first growing season is shown in figure A14. In the second year, average leaf length was 7.1 cm. *Achnatherum thurberianum* may extend the range of adaptation of the grasses as it appears adapted to more open, xeric habitats than the other grasses so might occupy drier microsites in the landscape.

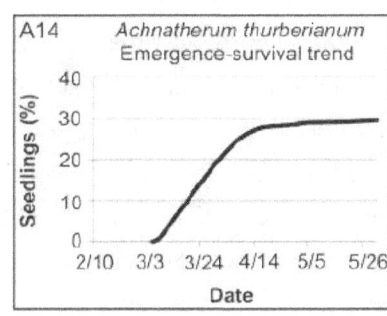

References

Archer (2000), Evans and Young (1978), Hitchcock (1951), Martens et al. (1994), USDA NRCS (2006). Young and Evans (1978).

Elymus elymoides (Raf.) Swezey
Bottlebrush squirrel tail
Poaceae
ELEL5

Elymus elymoides is a short-lived perennial grass with culms 1–50 cm tall, leaf blades are flat to involute, 5–20 cm long and 1–3 mm wide with soft whitish pubescence. The inflorescence, a spike, erect 2–7 cm long with widely spreading awns 2–10 cm long. Fruit are caryopses.

Distribution and habitat

Ranges from British Columbia to South Dakota, Missouri, Texas, California, and Mexico. Occurs in diverse dry habitat and ecotones of deserts, valleys, foothills, and mountain meadows at 610 to 3350 m (2,000 to 11,000 ft). Height varies with soil, moisture, and elevation. Early colonizer of disturbed sites but can be found in any of the successional stages. Cool-season species but tolerates full sun and drought. Can tolerate moderately saline or alkaline soils but grows poorly in granitic soils.

Reproductive ecology

Flowering occurs from late May through July. Species is wind pollinated but also self-fertile. Undamaged root crown will regenerate but new plants depend on seed dispersal. Self-fertilized seeds mature from June to September. The mean filled-seed rate of seeds collected from Green Ridge on the eastside central Oregon Cascade Range was 75.0 percent in 2004 and 81.8 percent in 2005.

Propagation

Seed heads were determined to be dry by the spreading of the awns from the rachis, which occurs as the plant dries, as determined by color change from green to pale yellow. Seed heads broke off the stem easily if the plant had cured. The long awns made it difficult to place into paper bags, so greater care was needed to ensure they stayed in the bags for drying and storage. Larger bags are recommended than those used for seed-only collections. Seeds are de-awned and cleaned using a Westrup machine with No. 14 screen twice through with hard brush. Screen with 1/18 by ¼ screen on Clipper with 2/3 air. Or can air blow at 25 mm with 2 by 24 screen. *Elymus elymoides* can produce large numbers of highly germinable seeds. The number of Green Ridge seeds per kilogram was 190,440 at 9.7 percent moisture content. When conditions are right, germination is rapid and stratification is not necessary. The mean germination rate of unstratified seeds collected from Green Ridge was 81 percent. Germination has been reported highest at night/day temperatures of 10/20 °C, (50/68 °F) but is inhibited at 20/30 °C (68/86 °F). Study seeds sown in furrows covered with soil in late September at Green Ridge germinated before February the following year (probably late fall) confirming that no stratification is needed. Germination based on accumulated emergence at the Green Ridge site was 62.8 percent. Mean survival by late May was 46.2 percent, and by May the following year, 15.3 percent. Trend in emergence and survival in the first year is shown in figure A15. Average herbceous cover of the subplot was 24 percent in May and 13 percent the following year. Cover per surviving individual actually increased because of height growth and tillering of surviving plants. Average height by May the second year was 9.1 cm. Results were excellent in growing out grass seed at Lucky Peak Nursery, Boise, Idaho, with 0.3 lb seed producing 2.74 lb the first year after sowing and 21.8 lb the following year.

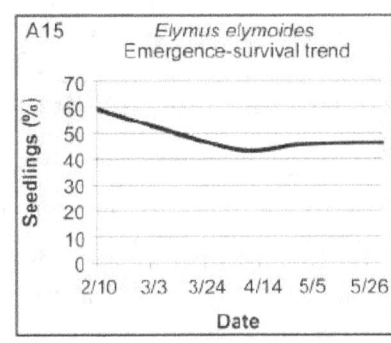

References

Beckstead et al. (1995), Hardegree et al. (2002), Harmond (1968), Hitchcock (1951), Jones (2006), O'Brien (1980), Rose et al. (1998), Simonin (2001), USDA NRCS (2006), USDI BLM (2003).

Festuca idahoensis Elmer
Idaho fescue
Poaceae
FEID

Festuca idahoensis is a cool-season, densely tufted, long-lived, perennial bunchgrass; with leaf blades that are scabrous, filiform, and involuted. Culms range widely in height (30–100 cm) with narrow panicles and 5–7 flowers in each spikelet with short awns (2–4 mm); fruit are caryopses. A typical bunchgrass with a caespitose growth form can reach 38 cm in diameter through clonal tillering.

Distribution and habitat

The range of *F. idahoensis* extends from British Columbia and Alberta south to California and Colorado. It is found in mountainous terrain growing commonly in rocky and open forests or grasslands at 300–4000 m elevations. *Festuca idahoensis* is a constant plant community member and indicator of the *Pinus ponderosa/Purshia tridentata/Festuca idahoensis* association. It is well adapted to coarse sandy loam but also grows in well-drained, coarse soils consisting of rock and sand. The species grows in a variety of light conditions from full light to partial shade and is drought tolerant.

Reproductive ecology

Although clonal spread through tillering is common, sexual reproduction through wind pollination is the primary mechanism for establishing new individuals. The species is long-lived and can persist as long as 60 years. Flowers are hermaphroditic and are wind pollinated. Sexual reproductive success can vary spatially and from year to year. The mean rate of filled seeds collected from Green Ridge on the east-side central Oregon Cascade Range was 47.0 percent in 2004 and 40.5 percent in 2005. Seeds mature in summer and disperse in July and August. In late summer, most of the seeds are dormant so that wetting by infrequent rainstorms will not cause them to germinate. However, seed germinates in late fall before the ground freezes and into late winter-early spring.

Propagation

Mature seeds are collected in mid summer. Mature flowering stems turn tan or light brown and lemmas separate or "fan out." Seeds are easily collected by hand just before they shed. The mean percentage of filled seeds collected at Green Ridge was 47.0 in 2004 and 40.5 in 2005. Seeds are cleaned using a Westrup machine with No. 12 screen run twice then air blown at 22 mm. A medium brush and No. 40 screen can be used and run twice on a Westrup machine. Screen with 1/16 by 1/4 cross-slot screen on Clipper with 1/4 air. The number of seeds per kilogram was 676,050 at 9.2 percent moisture content. Seed viability using tetrazolium was 83 percent, and germination rate of unstratified seeds under standard test conditions was 80.8 percent. Study seeds were sown at Green Ridge 1–2 cm deep in furrows in late September. Seeds germinated before winter and emerged by February. Based on accumulated emergence in the spring, germination of sown seeds was 48.1 percent. Peak emergence was in February with some attrition over the following months. Survival was 30.5 percent by May, and the following May, 9.5 percent. Trend in emergence and survival of seedlings over the first growing season is shown in figure A16. Average cover in the subplots was 11.3 percent in 2005 and 11.4 percent in 2006, an increase relative to the number of surviving seedlings because of tillering. Average leaf length was 8.3 cm by May of the second year. Results in growing out *F. idahoensis* for seed at Lucky Peak Nursery, Boise, Idaho, were good. About 0.08 lb of seed collected from Green Ridge produced 9.00 lb the second year after sowing.

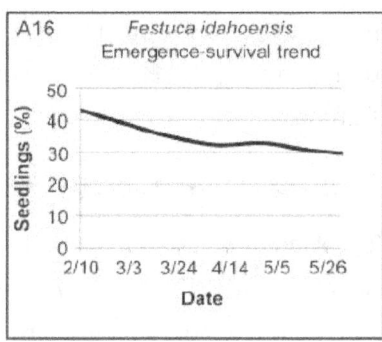

A16   *Festuca idahoensis* Emergence-survival trend

References

Doescher et al. (1985), Goodwin et al. (1995,1996), Harmond (1968), Hitchcock (1951), Johnson (1998), Liston et al. (2003), USDA NRCS (2006), USDI BLM (2003), Zouhar (2000).

Poa secunda Presl.
Sandberg bluegrass
Poaceae
POSE

Poa secunda is a short-lived, shallow-rooted, cool-season, perennial bunch-grass, part of a large complex of closely related grasses that differ ecologically and known collectively as Sandberg bluegrass. Culms erect, 30–50 cm, from a tuft of short, basal foliage. Blades short, soft, flat or folded. Panicle narrow, 2–10 cm long, spikelets spreading during anthesis 4–6 mm long, glumes acute, keeled; lemmas are without awns. Fruits are caryopses.

Distribution and habitat

Range is wide extending across western North America from Yukon south to southern California east to New Mexico and Nebraska. May be found in prairies, meadows, open forests, rocky slopes and mid to subalpine elevations growing in well-drained soils. Adapted to cold winters and dry, warm summers.

Reproductive ecology

The species is relatively short-lived, reproduction by seed. Wind pollinated, but also self-pollinated. *Poa secunda* is also apomictic (produces fertile seeds without pollination). Flowers wind pollinated but reported to attract flies. Flowering occurs mid to late May and seeds mature July–August. *Poa secunda* is known to hybridize with *P. pratensis* and *P. nervosa*. The rate of fertile seeds may not be high. Mean filled-seed rate of seeds collected from Green Ridge on east-side of central Oregon Cascade Range was 35.0 percent in 2004 and 33.2 percent in 2005.

Propagation

Poa secunda seeds are collected mid July–early August. Seeds are harvested by grasping the stem below the inflorescence and gently pulling upward, or by clipping the inflorescence. The mature seeds detach easily and are gathered in paper bags for transport to lab for further processing. Seeds are cleaned using a Westrup machine with medium brush and screen, hand screened with approximately 1/13 circular hand screen, and air blown, or screened with 1/13 round screen on Clipper and 1/4 air. The number of seeds collected from Green Ridge, Deschutes National Forest, per kilogram was 1,655,800 at 8.8 percent moisture content; viability by tetrazolium testing was 69 percent. Seed germination in the lab without stratification at 10 °C with 10 h light was 51.6 percent as reported by Deering and Young (2006). Germination of seeds sown in late September at Green Ridge based on accumulated emergence was 46.3 percent; mean survival by late May was 26.1 percent and by May the following year, 15.8 percent. Seeds germinated in late fall, and maximum germination had occurred by February. Note the trend in emergence and survival of seedlings during the first growing season shown in figure A17. Leaves grew slowly; median leaf length the second year was 3.7 cm. However, vegetative cover of the surviving seedlings increased from 1.0 to 5.7 percent because of tillering. Seeds collected from Green Ridge and sown at Lucky Peak Nursery, Boise, Idaho, resulted in 0.05 lb of seeds yielding 8.50 lb in the second year after sowing and 4.46 lb the third year for a total increase > 25,000 percent.

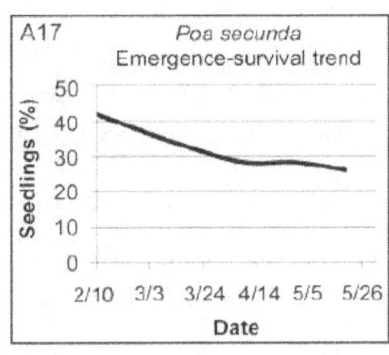

References

Darris (2007), Deering and Young (2006), Harmond (1968), Hitchcock (1951), Howard (1997), Rose et al. (1998), USDA NRCS (2006).

Pseudoroegneria spicata (Pursh.) A. Love
Bluebunch wheatgrass
Poaceae
PSSPS6

Pseudoroegneria spicata is a long-lived, cool-season, perennial grass. The leaves are narrow, flat or rolled, and slightly bluish-green. Culms are highly tufted, erect, almost wiry and 60–100 cm in height. Spike (flower head) is slender and upright, made up of stalkless spikelets up to six-flowered, glumes narrow, with lemma tipped by twisted awns half as long as spikelet.

Distribution and habitat

Range is throughout western North America from Alaska south through California and New Mexico, and from east of the Coast Range to Saskatchewan, Michigan, and Texas. *Pseudoroegneria spicata* ocurs in dry, open forest types, plains and prairies, on slopes, and open areas. The roots have a waxy covering that allows them to conserve moisture. May grow in full to partial sun; drought tolerant.

Reproductive ecology

Wind pollinated; however, seeds are highly self sterile; production of seeds and flowers does not occur every year. Propagates primarily by tillering but requires sexual reproduction for seed dispersal or repopulation after severe fire. Filled-seed percentages may vary from year to year. The mean rate of filled seeds from Green Ridge on the east side of the central Oregon Cascade Range was 33.3 percent in 2004 and 22.6 percent in 2005. This species' populations may be under-represented because of low fecundity and might benefit from supplementary seeding.

Propagation

Seeds are not easily harvested because seeds rapidly shed and few are filled. Seeds are collected by hand when they appear ready to shed, indicated by awns at right angles to stem and culm no longer green. The culm is grasped just below the inflorescence, bent 90 degrees, and gently pulled so that ripe seeds release into a paper bag. Seeds were cleaned using a Westrup machine with screen No. 13 or with hard brush and screen No. 12. Filled and empty seeds and chaff were separated with air at 18 mm or screened with 1/18 by 1/4 screen on Clipper and 2/3 air. Reported number of seeds per pound is

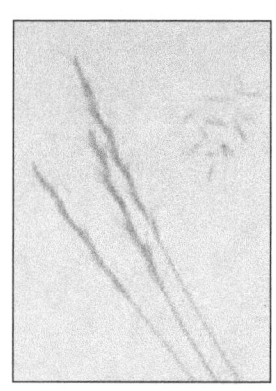

140,000; the number of Green Ridge seeds per kilogram was 267,790 at a moisture content of 9.3. Viability was 87 percent. The mean germination rate of unstratified seeds under standard conditions was 75.2 percent with about 10 percent moldy.

Seeds collected and sown at Green Ridge in the fall appeared to have germinated before winter. Germination based on accumulated emergence was 41.6 percent. Survival was 25.8 percent by the end of May. The trend in emergence and survival of seedlings at Green Ridge through the first growing season is shown in figure A18. Survival in May the following year was 6.4 percent; average leaf length of surviving seedlings was 10.0 cm. Cover in subplots decreased from 6.4 percent in 2005 to 4.1 percent but increased in proportion to the number of surviving seedlings because of height growth and tillering. In 2006, the plants had not yet produced culms. *Pseudoroegnaria spicata* usually reaches maturity in 2 to 3 years. Seeds collected from Green Ridge and sown at Lucky Peak Nursery, Boise, Idaho resulted in an excellent increase in seed with 0.25 lb of seeds yielding 3.50 lb in the second year and 0.81 lb in the third year for a total of 4.31 lb, an increase of > 1,500 percent.

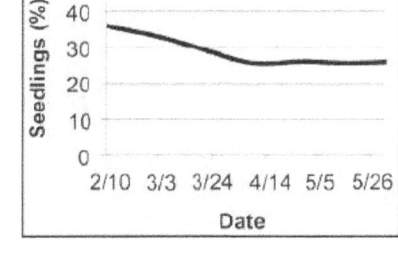

References

Hitchcock (1951), Ogle (2008), Rose et al. (1998), USDA FS (1937), USDA NRCS (2006), USDI BLM (2003), Zlatnik (1999).